Key Geography
Extensions

David Waugh with David Gardner

**Former Head of Geography
Trinity School, Carlisle**

**Head of Humanities and
ICT Coordinator, Raincliffe
School, Scarborough**

Stanley Thornes (Publishers) Ltd

First published in 1999 by:
Stanley Thornes (Publishers) Ltd
Ellenborough House
Wellington Street
CHELTENHAM GL50 1YW
England

00 01 02 03/ 10 9 8 7 6 5 4 3

A catalogue record for this book is available from the
British Library.

ISBN 0-7487-4066-X

Printed and bound in China by Dah Hua Printing
Press Co. Ltd

Designed and typeset by Hardlines, Charlbury, Oxford
Illustrated by Hardlines, Tim Smith and Angela Lumley
Picture research by Penni Bickle
Edited by Katherine James

Acknowledgements
With thanks to the following for permission to
reproduce photographs and other copyright material in
this book:

Action Aid, 80B; Aerofilms, 70C; Associated Press, 7G,
8C; Penni Bickle, 84A(2); Cephas/Kevin Judd, 115E;
Concern Worldwide, 81E; James Davis Travel
Photography, 87E(2), 110B, 113C, 115F, 120B(1), 123D,
124B, 126C; Eye Ubiquitous, 84A(5), 87E(1), 114C,
120B(2); Frank Lane Picture Agency, 10A, 13D, 17E,
22–23, 25H, 33C, 39D, 39E, 69E, 118B; David Gardner,
93D, 98C, 99F, 100A, 102A (1), 103C, 106A, 107D, 107E;
Geoscience Features, 10B, 11C, 37D, 41F, 66B; Eric and

David Hosking, Title page; Rosemary Humphries, 24D;
The Hutchison Library, 9E, 14E, 41E, 47G; New Zealand
Cards/Bob Beresford, 108C; Northumbrian Water, 21C;
Oxfam, 80C; Panos Pictures, 78A(1), 78B, 79D, 79F;
Emma Pole, 103C; Rex Features, 19D, 81F; Sealand
Aerial Photography, 71E, 75F; Peter Smith Photography,
24C, 54A, 93C, 93E; Pictorial Publications Ltd, 108D; Still
Pictures, 18A, 40C, 48D, 86C, 90C, 94A, 94B, 95D, 95E,
109E, 125G; Travel Ink, 69D; Ultra Photos/Yiorgos
Nikiteas, 14C, 56B, 66C, Stewart Weir, 74A–E, 78C, 79E;
US Geological Survey/EROS Data Center, Sioux Falls, SD,
88A, 88B; Tony Waltham/Geophotos, 16–17, 25I, 38B,
63C, 84A(1), 86D, 87E(3), 90B, 118D; Simon Warner,
15G, 24B, 24E, 24F, 66A; David Waugh, 64B, 64D–F, 114B,
115D, 118C, 118E, 119H, 119I, 123E, 125E, 125F; Judith
Waugh, 78A(1), 124C; Wildgoose Publications Ltd, 60A-D;
Simon Woodcock, 107E(1); Yorkshire Water, 92A.

Newcastle Chronicle and Journal Ltd, 21C; Philip Allan
Publishers (From Royle & Phillips, 'China's population
policy and its consequences', *Geography Review*, 11:1,
1997), 47F; Scarborough Evening News, 57E, 92B, 98D;
Telegraph Group Ltd, London, 1998, 20B.

Map extract 98A is taken from *Philip's Modern School
Atlas* 92nd Edition. Cartography by Philip's © George
Philip & Son Ltd.

Map extracts page 55, 60A-D, 70B, 71D, 97D and 99F are
reproduced from Ordnance Survey mapping with the
permission of The Controller of Her Majesty's Stationery
Office © Crown Copyright. Licence No. 07000U.

Every effort has been made to contact copyright
holders. The publishers apologise to anyone whose
rights have been inadvertently overlooked, and will be
happy to rectify any errors or omissions.

> **Note about the Internet links in *Extensions***
> Links to all the web sites referred to in *Extensions* are
> provided on the Stanley Thornes Key Geography web
> site. Simply type into your web browser:
>
>   http://www.thornes.co.uk/hmtl/keygeog/index.html
>
> This will allow you to link into all sites – regular
> updates will widen the range of links to the pupils'
> book. Remember to bookmark this site within your
> Internet browser. For ease of use you could create a
> separate folder called 'Key Geography' to save the link.
>
> The user should be aware that URLs or web addresses
> change quite frequently. Although every effort has
> been made to provide accurate addresses, it is
> inevitable that some will change. Updates of changes
> will be provided on the Key Geography web site.

Contents

Why is there a global pattern of earthquakes and volcanoes?

Two hundred million years ago there was only one landmass (diagram **A** i). About that time this landmass, known as Pangaea, began to split up. Initially this created two continental areas: Gondwanaland to the south, and Laurasia (diagram **A** ii). Further separation over millions of years has produced the continents, separated by oceans, as we know them today (diagram **A** iii). This movement of the continents, known as **continental drift**, is still continuing. Diagram **A** iv shows how scientists predict the world will look in 50 million years' time.

Since the Earth formed some 4,600 million years ago, its outer surface has cooled to form a thin **crust** (*Interactions* 28 diagram **A**). The crust lies on top of a molten layer of rock known as the **mantle**. The crust does not exist as a single piece but is broken into segments of varying sizes, called **plates** (*Interactions* 28 map **B**). Each plate floats, like a raft, on top of the mantle. Meanwhile, heat from within the Earth creates convection currents. Where these currents rise towards the surface, they cause the plates to move, perhaps by a few centimetres each year (diagram **B**). It is this movement that caused the break-up of Pangaea and results in continental drift (diagram **A**).

The place where two plates meet is called a **plate boundary** (or **margin**), and it is here that most of the world's earthquakes and volcanic eruptions occur. To understand why, you should be aware that there are two types of crust and four types of plate boundary.

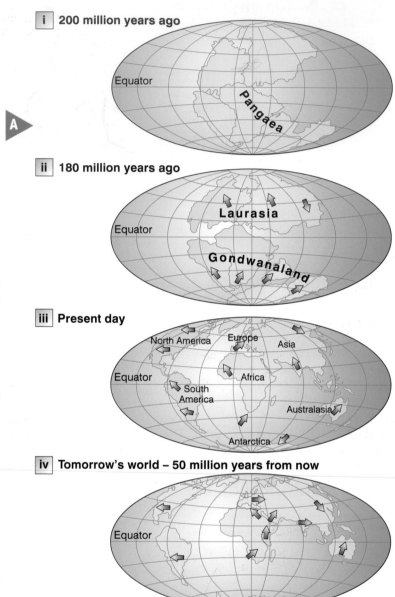

A

i | **200 million years ago**

Equator

Pangaea

ii | **180 million years ago**

Laurasia

Equator

Gondwanaland

iii | **Present day**

North America   Europe   Asia

Equator   Africa

South America

Australasia

Antarctica

iv | **Tomorrow's world – 50 million years from now**

Equator

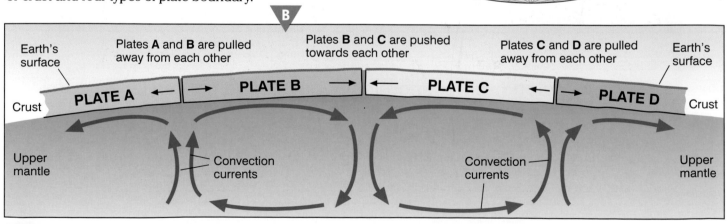

B

Earth's surface

Plates **A** and **B** are pulled away from each other

Plates **B** and **C** are pushed towards each other

Plates **C** and **D** are pulled away from each other

Earth's surface

Crust

PLATE A   →   →   PLATE B   →   ←   PLATE C   ←   →   PLATE D

Crust

Upper mantle

Convection currents

Convection currents

Upper mantle

1 Types of crust

Continental crust is lighter, it cannot sink and it is permanent (i.e. it is neither destroyed nor renewed). **Oceanic crust** is heavier, it can sink and it is continually being destroyed and renewed.

2 Types of plate boundary

Plates can either move away from, towards or sideways past neighbouring plates. These movements can create four different types of plate boundary (diagram **C**).

* A **constructive** boundary is where two plates move **away** from each other and new crust is **formed**.	* A **destructive** boundary is where two plates, **one** consisting of continental crust and **one** consisting of oceanic crust, move **towards** each other. As the oceanic crust is heavier it is pushed downwards and **destroyed**.
* A **conservative** boundary is where plates move **sideways past** each other. Crust is neither formed nor destroyed.	* A **collision** boundary is where two plates, **both** consisting of continental crust, move **towards** each other. As continental crust cannot sink, it is pushed upwards to form mountains and is neither formed nor destroyed.

C

D

Activities

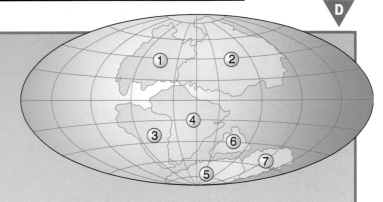

1 Diagram **D** shows the world as it was 180 million years ago. Name the present-day:
   a) continents (numbered 1 to 5) and
   b) countries (numbered 6 to 7).

2 Geographers are interested in patterns. Map **E** shows the location of the world's major earthquake zones and volcanic areas (see also *Interactions* 27 map **B** and 28 diagram **A**).
   a) Describe the pattern of earthquakes.
   b) Describe the pattern of volcanic activity.
   Remember: When describing patterns you should consider whether the distribution is even or uneven; whether it is linear (in lines) or clustered (in groups); occurs in the centre of continents, edges of continents or the middle of oceans. You should also give named examples, e.g. continents or oceans, to illustrate your points.
   c) In what ways are the patterns for earthquakes and volcanic areas:
   i) similar   ii) different?

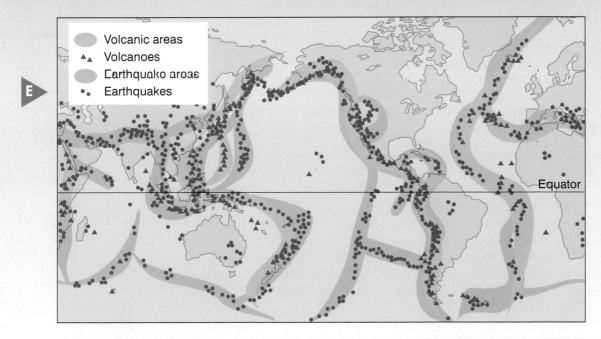

E

Legend:
- Volcanic areas
- ▲▲ Volcanoes
- Earthquake areas
- •. Earthquakes

Equator

What are the causes of earthquakes?

What is an earthquake?

An earthquake is a sudden movement, or tremor, in the Earth's crust. It is caused by the release of pressure which causes **shock** (or **seismic**) **waves**. The actual point in the crust where pressure is released, and which is therefore the centre of the earthquake, is known as the **focus**. The place on the Earth's surface directly above the focus is the **epicentre** (diagram **A**). It is at, or near to, the epicentre that the

Urban area – little damage, no loss of life

Strength of shock waves decreases

Sea-level/ground surface

Vertical section through the Earth's crust

EPICENTRE directly above the focus

Urban area – much damage and loss of life

FOCUS – centre of the earthquake

Shock waves spreading outwards

effects of the earthquake are likely to be the most severe. As the shock waves spread outwards from the focus they gradually decrease in strength and, as a result, places on the Earth's surface further away from the epicentre experience less damage and loss of life.

How are earthquakes measured?

Shock (or seismic) waves are recorded by a sensitive instrument called a **seismograph** (diagram **B**), while the strength of an earthquake is measured on the **Richter scale** (diagram **C**). The scale can, at first glance, be misleading because each point is ten times greater than the previous one. So an earthquake registering 7 on the scale is actually ten times greater than one measuring 6, and 100 times greater than one measuring 5.

A seismograph reading

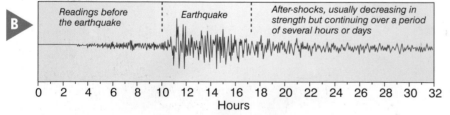

Readings before the earthquake

Earthquake

After-shocks, usually decreasing in strength but continuing over a period of several hours or days

0 2 4 6 8 10 12 14 16 18 20 22 24 26 28 30 32
Hours

What are the causes of earthquakes?

Earthquakes occur where there are weaknesses and movements in the Earth's crust. *Interactions* 27 map **B** shows the epicentres of many of the most recent earthquakes. You will notice that most of these have occurred at, or near to, plate boundaries (*Interactions* 28 map **B**). However, those at constructive margins are usually much less destructive than those at collision (diagram **D**), destructive (diagram **E**) and conservative (diagram **F**) margins.

RICHTER SCALE

Examples	Possible effects
About 150,000 recorded earth movements a year – nearly all undetected by people	Only detected by seismographs
10,000 or so earth movements felt by people	Faint tremors, no damage
	Doors and windows rattle
	Chimney-pots fall, plaster cracks
Afghanistan 1998 *6.1*	Poorly-built houses collapse
San Francisco 1989 *6.9*	Major quake. Large concrete buildings collapse
Kobe 1995 *7.2*	
Mexico City 1985 *7.8*	Many buildings collapse. Bridges destroyed. Gaps in ground
San Francisco 1906 *8.2*	
Lisbon 1755 *8.8* (largest recorded earthquake)	Total destruction. Ground rises and falls

1 2 3 4 5 6 7 8 9 10 11 12

Top of scale

D
At collision plate boundaries

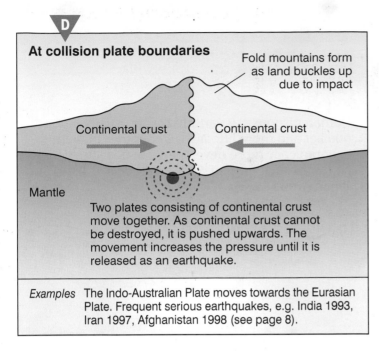

Fold mountains form as land buckles up due to impact

Continental crust   Continental crust

Mantle

Two plates consisting of continental crust move together. As continental crust cannot be destroyed, it is pushed upwards. The movement increases the pressure until it is released as an earthquake.

Examples   The Indo-Australian Plate moves towards the Eurasian Plate. Frequent serious earthquakes, e.g. India 1993, Iran 1997, Afghanistan 1998 (see page 8).

G
People are often left homeless after an earthquake

E
At destructive plate boundaries (*Interactions* 29)

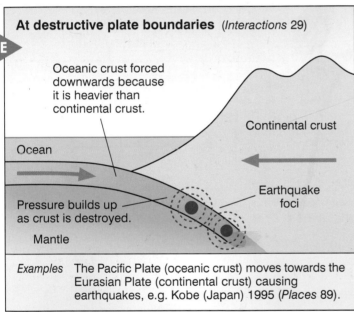

Oceanic crust forced downwards because it is heavier than continental crust.

Continental crust

Ocean

Earthquake foci

Pressure builds up as crust is destroyed.

Mantle

Examples   The Pacific Plate (oceanic crust) moves towards the Eurasian Plate (continental crust) causing earthquakes, e.g. Kobe (Japan) 1995 (*Places* 89).

F
At conservative plate boundaries

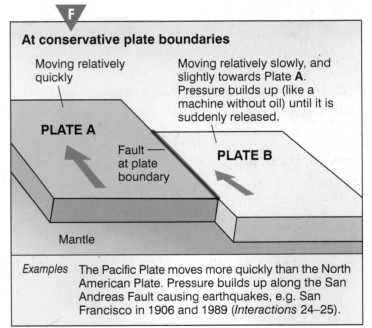

Moving relatively quickly

Moving relatively slowly, and slightly towards Plate **A**. Pressure builds up (like a machine without oil) until it is suddenly released.

PLATE A

Fault at plate boundary

PLATE B

Mantle

Examples   The Pacific Plate moves more quickly than the North American Plate. Pressure builds up along the San Andreas Fault causing earthquakes, e.g. San Francisco in 1906 and 1989 (*Interactions* 24–25).

Activities

1   As a geographer you should be building up your geographical vocabulary. Write down the meaning of the following terms:
   a) earthquake focus   **b)** epicentre
   c) seismic waves.

2   With reference to diagram **B**, how many times stronger was the 1906 San Francisco earthquake than those in:
   a) Japan (Kobe) in 1995
   b) Afghanistan in 1998?

3   **a)** Twelve earthquakes are named on *Interactions* 27 map **B**. Name those located on:
      i)   collision plate boundaries
      ii) destructive plate boundaries
      iii) conservative plate boundaries.
   b) Why do so many earthquakes occur at plate boundaries?

4   If you have access to the Internet, look up

   http://geology.usgs.gov

   which will give you the latest information on earthquakes.

How do people respond to earthquakes?

Both the effects of earthquakes, and people's responses to them, vary between different parts of the world. As a generalisation:

- The effects of earthquakes are usually much greater in countries that are economically less developed – that is, 'poorer' countries such as Iran (1997) and Afghanistan (1998).

- Human response to earthquakes is usually much quicker and more effective in countries that are economically more developed – that is, the 'richer' countries such as the USA (San Francisco 1989) and Japan (Kobe 1995).

Case Study

Afghanistan 1998

On 4 February an earthquake measuring 6.1 on the Richter scale occurred in the remote northern Afghanistan province of Takhar (map **A**). The area was so remote that it took three days for news of the event to reach Kabul, the Afghan capital. The extracts in figure **C** were taken from British newspapers and from the Internet.

A

B

People waiting in freezing temperatures for UN aid to arrive – 14 February 1998

C

7 February
Reports are coming in of a severe earthquake in northern Afghanistan.

8 February
A relief team from Médécins Sans Frontière claim that over 20 known villages in the Rostaq region have been destroyed and that the death total could exceed 4,000. It has taken it, and another relief team from the Red Crescent, many hours' travelling by donkey and horse, as most of the rough mountain tracks have either been destroyed by landslides triggered by the earthquake or are blocked by snow.

9 February
Urgent food and medical supplies have still not reached the region due to a combination of poor weather (which has prevented helicopters from flying), blocked mountain tracks (further snowfall and landslides) and the local civil war.

10 February
Relief agencies have flights of aid ready but are being constantly held back by bad weather (fog and further snowfalls). Reports suggest that survivors are having to live without shelter in sub-zero temperatures and that thousands are facing starvation if they remain in the region. Already hundreds of villagers are trundling down muddy tracks carrying heavy bundles and leading their goat herds.

16 February
Helicopters have at last managed to drop supplies to three isolated villages 11 days after the earthquake. Latest figures suggest that 27 villages have been totally or largely destroyed, 4,000 people have died, 10,000 injured and 15,000 made homeless. So far 4,800 blankets, 220 tents, 800 quilts, 1,500 tonnes of food and 1.7 tonnes of medical kits have been received.

Can people predict earthquakes?

The simple answer is 'No', although scientists can:
- use sensitive instruments to measure increases in earth movements and/or a build-up of pressure
- map the epicentres and frequency of previous earthquakes to see if there is either a repeat location or a time-interval pattern.

Even so, this may only indicate the possible timing of an event (and then not within ten years) and certainly not its precise location.

A third, and non-scientific, indicator is animal behaviour. It appears that some animals behave in unpredictable and unusual ways before an earthquake, for example fish jumping, dogs howling, or mice and rats fleeing from houses.

Can people plan for earthquakes?

Attempts can be made, especially in richer places such as California and Japan, to:
- construct buildings and roads to withstand earthquakes (diagram **D** and photo **E**)
- have emergency services trained and available, e.g. helicopters, ambulances and fire engines.

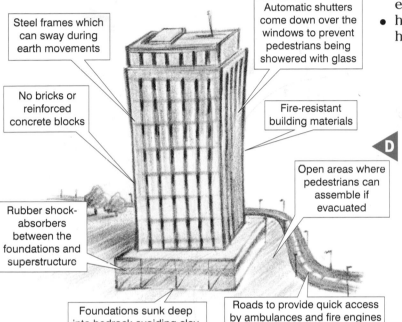

Steel frames which can sway during earth movements

Automatic shutters come down over the windows to prevent pedestrians being showered with glass

No bricks or reinforced concrete blocks

Fire-resistant building materials

Rubber shock-absorbers between the foundations and superstructure

Open areas where pedestrians can assemble if evacuated

Foundations sunk deep into bedrock avoiding clay

Roads to provide quick access by ambulances and fire engines

D

E

Activities

1 With reference to page 7, explain why earthquakes often occur in Afghanistan.

2 **a)** Complete table **F** by using material on page 8 of this book and *Interactions* 24–25, to show how the effects of an earthquake can differ between a developed country and a developing country.
   b) Which of the two earthquakes had the higher measurement on the Richter scale?
   c) Why were there so many more deaths and injuries in Afghanistan than in San Francisco?
   d) Why was aid received:
      i) within hours in San Francisco
      ii) only after several days in Afghanistan?

3 **a)** What can people do to predict earthquakes? How successful are these predictions?
   b) What can be done to lessen the effects of earthquakes? Why are such attempts more likely to be successful in richer countries?

F

Earthquake location	San Francisco 1989 A city in a developed country	Takhar 1998 A region in a developing country
Population density	High	Low
Measurement on the Richter scale	6.9	
Estimated deaths	67	
Estimated injuries		
Estimated homeless	2,000	
Types of damage		
Causes of death		

What are the causes of volcanic eruptions?

Volcanoes are cone-shaped mountains formed by the ejection of material, often at irregular intervals. They are likely to occur where there are weaknesses in the Earth's crust and where **magma**, which is molten rock, rises to the surface. When a volcano erupts, magma is forced upwards through a **vent** (an opening in the Earth's crust) to the **crater** (a funnel-shaped hollow at the summit of a volcano). The magma may flow out of the crater as **lava** (molten rock) or be ejected more violently as **volcanic bombs** (large fragments of rock), **ash** and **dust** (photo **A**, and *Interactions* 20 diagram **A**).

Map **E** on page 5 shows the location of the world's more important volcanoes. At first glance it may seem that most of these occur at, or near to, plate boundaries (*Interactions* 28 map **B**). A closer inspection will show that volcanoes occur at only two of the four types of plate boundary (table **C** on page 5) – that is, the constructive (figure **B**) and destructive (figure **C**) margins.

A

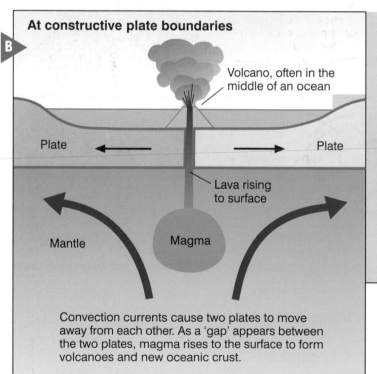

At constructive plate boundaries

B

Volcano, often in the middle of an ocean

Plate

Plate

Lava rising to surface

Mantle

Magma

Convection currents cause two plates to move away from each other. As a 'gap' appears between the two plates, magma rises to the surface to form volcanoes and new oceanic crust.

Examples

The North American Plate moves away from the Eurasian Plate. The movement allows magma to reach the surface where, as lava, it forms volcanic islands (Iceland, Canary Islands) and new oceanic crust (diagram **D** page 5).

The island of Surtsey was formed off the coast of Iceland in 1963

Volcanoes at constructive plate margins usually:

- have fairly gentle eruptions
- consist mainly of lava
- are relatively low in height
- have gently sloping sides because the lava, coming from the mantle, is 'runny' and can flow a considerable distance before cooling and solidifying.

At destructive plate boundaries

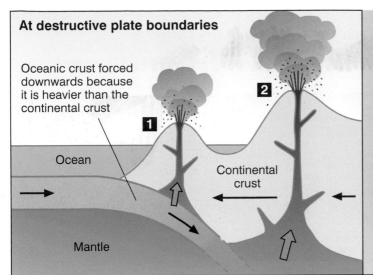

Oceanic crust forced downwards because it is heavier than the continental crust

Ocean

1

2

Continental crust

Mantle

As oceanic crust is forced downwards it is destroyed due to heat caused by friction between the continental crust and the oceanic crust, and heat from the mantle. As the crust turns to magma, the molten rock rises to the surface to form:

1 offshore islands (island arcs)

2 volcanoes within coastal mountain ranges

Examples

1 The Pacific Plate and the Philippines Plate move towards the Eurasian Plate forming the island arcs of Japan (*Places* 88) and the Philippines (Pinatubo).

2 The Nazca Plate moves towards the South American Plate, creating volcanoes in the Andes.

Volcanoes at destructive plate margins usually:

- have very violent eruptions
- consist of lava, volcanic bombs, dust and ash
- are often very high
- have steep sides as rock and ash build up around the crater, and lava, coming from destroyed oceanic crust, does not flow far before cooling and solidifying.

C

Activities

1 As a geographer you should be building up your geographical vocabulary. Write down the meanings of the following terms:
  a) vent   **b)** crater   **c)** magma
  d) lava   **e)** volcanic bombs.

2 a) 12 volcanoes were named on *Interactions* 26 map **A**. Make a list of those located on:
  i) constructive plate boundaries
  ii) destructive plate boundaries.
  b) Why do so many volcanoes occur at constructive and destructive plate boundaries?
  c) Copy and complete table **D** to show the differences between volcanoes found at constructive and destructive plate boundaries.

3 a) If you have access to the Internet, look up Volcano World at

  http://volcano.und.nodak.edu

  which will give you the latest information on volcanic eruptions.

b) On a map of the world, plot the location of the most recent eruptions.

D

	Constructive plate boundary	Destructive plate boundary
Direction in which the two plates involved move		
Source of lava		
Type of material ejected		
Strength of eruption		
Shape of volcanoes		
Height of volcanoes		
Examples		

How do people respond to volcanic eruptions?

People are often attracted to volcanic areas. This is partly because lava soon weathers into a fertile soil and partly because volcanic areas can attract tourists (e.g. sightseers and skiers) and provide geothermal power. Some volcanoes, such as Etna, erupt frequently and people living on their slopes accept the risk. Others, such as Pinatubo, had not erupted for so long that people no longer believed that there was a risk.

Usually a volcano shows increasing signs of activity before it actually erupts. This means that people usually have sufficient time to save themselves and their animals, if not their property. Indeed, although there are cases of ash and mudflows destroying towns and killing the inhabitants, it is often the after-effects, such as tidal waves and disease, that cause most deaths (table **A**).

Eruption/date	Perceived risk	Effects
Vesuvius (Italy) AD 79	None – not known to be a volcano	20,000 deaths. Towns of Pompeii (ash) and Herculaneum (mud) destroyed
Krakatoa (Indonesia) 1883	None – uninhabited	One-third of island blown away but no deaths. Resultant tidal wave killed 36,000
Mount St Helens (USA) 1980	Low – dormant for 120 years	61 deaths due to gases and mudflows
Pinatubo (Philippines) 1991	Fairly low. No eruption for 600 years. Good area for farming	700 deaths – 6 due to eruption (gases), 70 to mudflows. Over 600 die from disease
Etna (Sicily) every few years	Very high but ideal for farming and tourism	Usually no deaths – occasional damage to buildings, e.g. farms, ski-lift, observatory

A

Case Study

Montserrat 1995–98

The Caribbean island of Montserrat (102 km²), formed at a destructive plate boundary, is dominated by the Soufrière Hills volcano (map **B**). As the volcano had been dormant for over 400 years, local people no longer considered it to be a risk and many farmed its lower slopes. All this changed when, in July 1995, steam was reported to be rising from the volcano's crater. The extracts in figure **C** were taken from British newspapers and the Internet.

B

NORTH AMERICA

SOUTH AMERICA

Montserrat

Caribbean Sea

Central Hills — Airport

Salem

Montserrat

N

Plymouth (capital)

Soufrière Hills 914 m

0 — 4
Kilometres

• Villages

Late 1995
Ash has begun to fall on Plymouth, the island's capital. With forecasts of further eruptions, the inhabitants of Plymouth have been evacuated to a 'safe zone' in the north (diagram **E**).

September 1996
Magma, rising up the vent, created a dome which was eventually removed by a violent explosion. Rivers of ash, mud, rock and hot gases swept down the mountainside in all directions. The airport has been destroyed.

Early 1997
Some people have returned home, against official advice, as the volcano seems to be less active.

January 1998
Activity at its quietest for 2½ years.

June 1997
A huge explosion caused mudflows which flowed downhill at over 100 km/hour. The mudflows overran several villages killing 19 people, including some who had returned home. Ash has even fallen in the Safe Zone.

August 1997
Further eruptions have caused lava and mud to reach Plymouth. By now over 80% of buildings have been destroyed (mainly by fire) and ash is 1.25 m thick (photo **D**). The Danger Zone has been extended to include Salem.

July 1998
Major eruption caused ash to fall on surrounding islands.

C

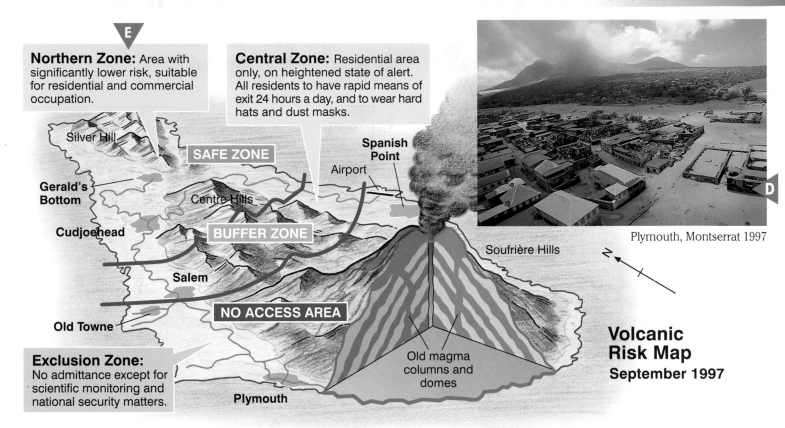

Northern Zone: Area with significantly lower risk, suitable for residential and commercial occupation.

Central Zone: Residential area only, on heightened state of alert. All residents to have rapid means of exit 24 hours a day, and to wear hard hats and dust masks.

Silver Hill

SAFE ZONE

Gerald's Bottom

Centre Hills

Cudjoehead

BUFFER ZONE

Salem

Spanish Point

Airport

Soufrière Hills

NO ACCESS AREA

Old Towne

Old magma columns and domes

Exclusion Zone: No admittance except for scientific monitoring and national security matters.

Plymouth

Plymouth, Montserrat 1997

Volcanic Risk Map
September 1997

Can people predict volcanic eruptions?

Scientists can often give some warning that an eruption is imminent. They can do this by:

- using instruments to measure any rise in pressure, increase in seismic activity (earth tremors), release of gases or, sometimes, even changes in the shape of a volcano
- studying:
  i) pre-eruption activity to see if there is a repeat of earlier patterns
  ii) post-eruption activity to see if lava and mudflows follow set routes
  iii) previous eruptions to see if they have occurred at regular intervals, e.g. in the West Indies a major eruption seems to occur, on average, every 30–40 years – unfortunately there are over 25 active volcanoes in the area and scientists cannot accurately say which one will be next, or when.

Activities

1 a) Why do some people live in areas at risk from volcanic eruptions?
   b) What can scientists do to predict volcanic eruptions?
   c) How successful are these predictions?

2 Describe how the eruption of *either* Soufrière Hills volcano (Montserrat), *or* Etna (*Interactions* 22–23) *or* any other volcano that you have studied, affected the lives of people living in the area.

3 Scientists working in Montserrat predict that over the next few years:
   - there is a 20 per cent chance that eruptions will slowly die away
   - there is a 60 per cent chance that eruptions will remain the same as they have been since 1995
   - there is a 20 per cent chance that there will be a really violent eruption.
   How will **each** of these three predictions affect:
   a) the south of Montserrat
   b) the central Buffer Zone
   c) the north of Montserrat?

4 If you have access to the Internet, it is possible to keep up to date with the latest developments of the Soufrière Hills eruption by visiting the web site of the Government of Montserrat and the Montserrat Volcano Observatory at:

   http:/www.geo.mtu.edu/volcanoes/west.indies/soufriere/govt

How does rock type and weathering affect the development of landforms?

Rock type

The Earth's crust consists of many different types of rock. It is usual to group (**classify**) these rocks into three main types. This simple grouping (**classification**) is based upon how each type of rock is formed (table **A**).

The **resistance** (or hardness) of a rock affects the development of landforms. The harder the rock, the more resistant it will be to erosion. This means that hills and mountains usually consist of harder rock, while lowlands develop in areas of softer rock.

Rock type	Formation	Examples
Igneous	Volcanic activity – consists of crystals	Granite, basalt
Sedimentary	Laid down in layers	Sandstone, chalk, limestone
Metamorphic	Changed by extremes of heat and pressure	Marble, slate

A

Drainage basins and rivers

In a drainage basin (see page 17), valley sides are likely to be steeper (photo **B**) where the rock is more resistant (harder), and more gentle (photo **C**) where the rock is less resistant (softer). Where bands of harder rock cross a valley, they are likely to create waterfalls and rapids (page 16; *Connections* 10–11 and 97).

Coasts

On coasts, resistant rocks form steep cliffs and headlands while less resistant, softer rocks are more easily eroded to give bays (diagram **D** and photo **E**; *Connections* 14).

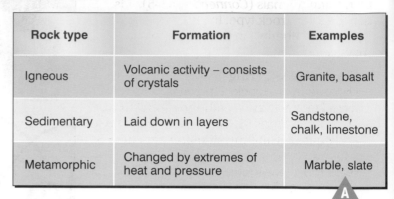

B

C

E

D

Less resistant, softer rock

Resistant, harder rock

Waves approaching the land

Less resistant, softer rock

Resistant, harder rock

Original coastline

Present-day coastline

Weathering

Weathering is when rocks are broken down in the place where they were formed by the action of weather and, to a lesser extent, by plants and animals (*Connections* 4–5). It is usual, as with rock type, to group the various types of weathering, in this case into two main categories.

1 **Physical weathering** is when force is used to break up the rock. The force may come from **freeze–thaw** weathering (photo **F** and *Connections* 4), from extremes of heat and cold (**exfoliation** or onion weathering – *Connections* 4), or from the action of plant roots (**biological** weathering – *Connections* 5).

2 **Chemical weathering** is when a chemical change takes place in a rock. Two examples of chemical weathering are when:
   - oxygen turns rocks that contain iron into a reddish-brown colour (rust)
   - rainwater containing acids such as carbonic acid (which is liquid carbon dioxide) dissolves rocks that consist of calcium carbonate (limestone and chalk – photo **G** and *Connections* 5).

Once rock has been weathered and broken down, it can be transported to different places by rivers, the sea, the wind and by ice.

Activities

1 Have you remembered how to draw landsketches? (If not, check *Foundations* 10–11.)
   a) Draw landsketches for photos **B** and **C**.
   b) On the appropriate sketch, and in suitable places, add the following labels:
      - hard, resistant rock
      - softer, less resistant rock
      - gentle valley sides
      - steep valley sides
      - wide valley floor
      - narrow valley floor
      - deep valley
      - shallow valley.
   c) Give each landsketch a title.

2 Using diagram **D** and photo **E**, write a paragraph to explain the formation of headlands and bays.

3 Refer to *Connections* 15 map **D**, which shows part of the coastline of Yorkshire. The map does not actually tell you that there are cliffs along this coastline from Flamborough Head almost to Spurn Head. How then does the map suggest to you that the cliffs at Flamborough Head are made of resistant rock and the cliffs between Bridlington and Hornsea are made of less resistant rock?

4 a) What is meant by the term 'weathering'?
   b) What is the difference between 'physical weathering' and 'chemical weathering'?

What are the main processes that produce river landforms?

EROSION

The wearing away of the land by material carried by a river followed by the removal of loose material (boulders, rock and soil)

Processes

1. When material is moved along the river bed and it collides with other material, causing it to break into smaller pieces (**attrition**).

2. When fine material carried by a river rubs against the banks, acting like sandpaper (**abrasion**).

3. When certain rocks are dissolved by acids in the river (**solution** or **corrosion**).

4. When the sheer force of the river hits its banks (**hydraulic action**).

TRANSPORTATION

The picking up and movement of eroded material by a river

Processes

1. Large rocks and boulders can be rolled along the river bed (**traction**).

2. Smaller stones can be 'bounced' along the river bed (**saltation**).

3. Fine material (**sand** and **silt**) can be picked up and carried within the river (**suspension**).

4. Material can be dissolved and carried by the river (**solution**).

Landforms

1. V–shaped valleys (*Connections 8–9*).
2. Waterfalls and rapids (*Connections 10–11, 97*).
3. Outside of a meander (*Connections 12–13*).

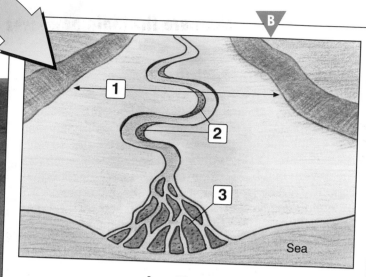

DEPOSITION

The dropping and laying down of material carried by a river

Occurs

1. When river levels fall (e.g. after a spell of dry weather) and the river can no longer carry so much material.

2. When the river slows down (at the inside of a bend or where it meets the sea) so that, again, the river cannot carry much material.

B

Sea

Landforms

1. Flood plains (*Connections* 13, 88 and 96).
2. Inside of a meander (*Connections* 12–13).
3. Deltas (*Connections* 88).

D

Activities

1. Diagram **C** is an incomplete sketch of a **river** (or **drainage**) **basin** (*Foundations* 30). Make a copy and add to it, in appropriate places, the following labels:
   - drainage basin
   - watershed
   - source
   - tributary
   - mouth
   - neighbouring drainage basin.

2. **a)** What is the difference between erosion, transportation and deposition?
   b) Briefly describe the processes by which a river may erode its banks and bed.
   c) Briefly describe the processes by which a river may transport material.
   d) Under what conditions may a river deposit material?

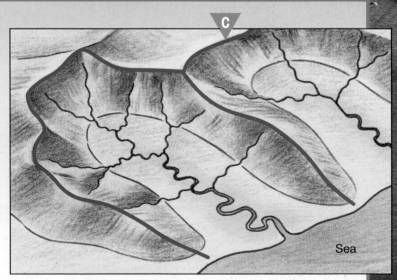

C

Sea

What are the causes and effects of river floods?

Frequency and prediction

Some drainage basins, like that of the Ganges and Brahmaputra in India and Bangladesh (*Foundations 32–33*), experience river floods each year. Indeed, people living in such places have come to rely upon the annual flood. Other drainage basins, such as the Severn in the UK, experience less frequent flooding. Here the timing of the flood is irregular, it cannot be predicted and it often disrupts human activity (photo **A**). In still other drainage basins, for example the Lavant at Chichester in 1994, flooding is not expected and so, when it does occur, it takes everyone by surprise.

A

Causes

Many rivers have always flooded. This is due to **natural** causes such as relief, rock type and extremes of climate (diagram **B**). However, many of these rivers, and an increasing number of those previously not prone to flooding, now flood both more frequently and to a greater extent. In most cases this is due to **human** mismanagement within the drainage basin (diagram **C**).

C

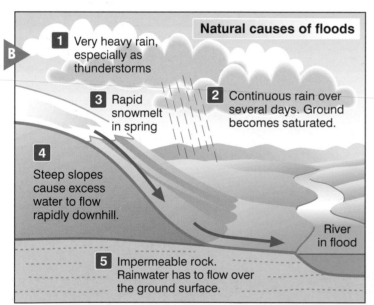

B

Natural causes of floods

1 Very heavy rain, especially as thunderstorms

2 Continuous rain over several days. Ground becomes saturated.

3 Rapid snowmelt in spring

4 Steep slopes cause excess water to flow rapidly downhill.

River in flood

5 Impermeable rock. Rainwater has to flow over the ground surface.

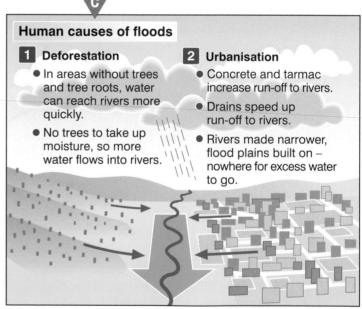

Human causes of floods

1 **Deforestation**
- In areas without trees and tree roots, water can reach rivers more quickly.
- No trees to take up moisture, so more water flows into rivers.

2 **Urbanisation**
- Concrete and tarmac increase run-off to rivers.
- Drains speed up run-off to rivers.
- Rivers made narrower, flood plains built on – nowhere for excess water to go.

Activities

1 a) Under what natural conditions might you expect a river to flood? Give your answer under the headings:
   i) climate   ii) relief and rock type.

b) Explain how human activities have increased the risk of river floods.

Effects

Flooding can, at its best, provide fertile silt for fields and water for crops. At its worst, flooding can cause loss of life (both people and animals), destruction of property and crops, and the disruption of communications and economic activities.

Case Study

English Midlands, Easter 1998

April began very wet. Within the first few days many places in the Midlands received twice as much rainfall as they would normally expect in a whole month. The ground was, therefore, saturated before Thursday 8 April. On that one day, Peterborough had a normal month's rainfall, while places in the Avon Valley, to the west, had over 50 mm of rain. At Stratford, the River Avon rose by 2.5 metres in just two hours. Elsewhere, the Environment Agency issued 75 red warning alerts on more than 30 rivers. What followed was the worst flooding in the region for over 50 years (photo **D** and map **E**).

- People had to be evacuated or rescued from houses as far apart as Banbury, Leamington, Newport Pagnell, Northampton and Evesham.
- Many towns and villages were cut off.
- At Stratford, the Avon flooded the Royal Shakespeare Theatre to a depth of 4 metres.
- Hundreds of people were delayed as train services to the North-west and motorways such as the M40 were flooded. The situation was made worse as it was the Thursday before the Easter weekend.
- Five deaths were reported, four by drowning and one from hypothermia.
- Estimates put the bill for damage at £1.5 billion.

D

E

2 **a)** Give two possible advantages and three possible disadvantages of river floods.

b) Describe i) the causes and ii) the effects of the floods in the English Midlands at Easter 1998.

c) Describe i) the similarities and ii) the differences between the flood in the English Midlands, and *either*:

- the 1988 flood in Bangladesh (*Foundations* 32), *or*
- the 1994 flood in northern Italy (*Places* 80), or
- any other flood that you have studied (this may be from watching the TV, reading newspaper accounts or using the Internet).

What can people do to try to control river floods?

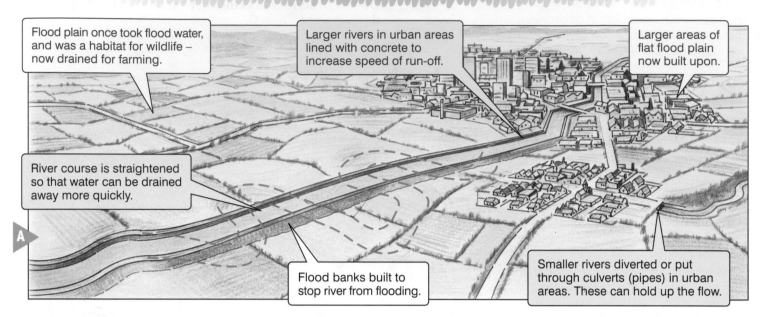

Flood plain once took flood water, and was a habitat for wildlife – now drained for farming.

Larger rivers in urban areas lined with concrete to increase speed of run-off.

Larger areas of flat flood plain now built upon.

River course is straightened so that water can be drained away more quickly.

Flood banks built to stop river from flooding.

Smaller rivers diverted or put through culverts (pipes) in urban areas. These can hold up the flow.

Until recently it was thought that the best way to prevent rivers from flooding was to put them into artificial channels. This was done at a time when flood plains were being increasingly built upon for urban development, and drained for farming and recreation (diagram **A**).

Recent floods, including those in the English Midlands (pages 18–19), have led many people to realise that complete river and flood control is impossible. Although the frequency of flooding may be reduced, when there are extremes of weather, the adverse effects are often much greater. Increasingly, bad planning is being blamed for flooding (figure **B**).

Flooding 'is caused by poor planning'

By Charles Clover, Environment Editor

THE Easter floods were described as 'a predicted man-made crisis' by a conservationist yesterday as the Environment Agency called on planners to reject more applications to build in areas prone to flooding.

The agency, which spends £250 million – half its budget – on flood defence and early warning systems to protect the six million people who live in flood-prone areas, warned that further development on low-lying areas beside rivers would lead to more flooded homes and increased costs for the taxpayer.

Robin Page, the conservationist and *Daily Telegraph* columnist, said the Easter floods in Bedfordshire, Northamptonshire and Cambridgeshire were a result of misguided planning decisions and flood defence schemes

by the Environment Agency or its predecessors.

'We have been predicting floods of this sort for years. The floods were caused in the main by absurd drainage and planning policies. For 30 years drainage engineers have been turning our rivers and streams into flushing mechanisms. By deepening the channels they have speeded up and increased the flow of water from the land.

In wet weather the flow should be slowed down, the surplus water should be on the flood plains not flushed at high speeds seawards, threatening all the towns downstream. Incredibly the problems of Bedford, Northampton, Peterborough and Huntingdon have been made worse by planners building on flood plains.'

He said that land east of Bedford had been heightened and built on, which had led to flooding to the north and west.

Dr Geoff Mance, of the Environment Agency, said: 'Settlement was naturally attracted to flood-plain areas and river corridors, but only in recent years, as the extent and rate of development increased, have the risks come to be recognised.

Only now are we coming to accept that it is more cost-effective, in environmental as well as financial terms, to work with nature rather than to fight against it.'

The Daily Telegraph, 18 April 1998

The causes of the English Midlands flood of Easter 1998

The latest approach to river management is the growing acceptance that, as floods are part of the river's natural cycle, then flooding should be allowed as a natural event. Such an approach would:

- be far less expensive than constructing large-scale flood prevention schemes
- improve water quality and re-create wildlife habitats.

One such scheme, on the River Skerne in Darlington, is described in figure **C**.

Case Study

Flowing tributes for a river

YESTERDAY, a conference was held in Darlington to tell the story of the restoration of a 2 km stretch of the Skerne through the town centre and to mark the completion of a £1 million venture. The project, started three years ago, was to transform a stretch of a town-centre river from being a straight, virtually lifeless engineered canal to a meandering waterway rich in habitats.

The idea for the project first emerged in 1990 when a Swedish professor outlined the theory of restoring rivers at a conference in York.

The main players have been Northumbrian Water, Darlington Council and the Environment Agency, which gained access to European funds.

The challenge in Darlington was to undo the damage caused in the days when industrialised, growing centres saw water only as a raw material and rivers as a way of getting rid of pollution.

Years of industrial tipping had raised the land around the river, which had been forced into a rigid canal-like shape to counter flooding.

Tonnes of earth were excavated to lower the flood plain and create a situation that was safer than the old canal solution.

New look: The Skerne with its newly-created meanders and range of wildlife habitats

The river's curves were recreated and pools and backwaters fashioned to provide a range of habitats. The river's former straight sides which fell vertically to the water, and on which nothing lived, were replaced by slopes.

Rapid flow areas were introduced by the use of stone and gravel. This helps oxygenate the water and allows people to hear the rippling and bubbling of the river.

After nearly 400 tonnes of rubbish was hauled out of the water, more than 20 ugly concrete drains feeding into the river were tackled.

The transformation is remarkable. Newcomers would assume it has always looked as it does now. The whole project has been written up in great detail so that it can be used as a blueprint for other places.

As it was: The straight and almost lifeless River Skerne

Newcastle Journal, 11 July 1998

Activities

1 **a)** Describe, in a short paragraph, the ways in which people used to try to control rivers and to prevent flooding.
   b) What were:
      i) the advantages and
      ii) the disadvantages of these methods?

2 **a)** Why do an increasing number of people now believe that rivers should be allowed to flood?
   b) Briefly describe how their ideas have been applied to the River Skerne.

3 Name a river or stream near to where you live.
   a) How often does it flood? (frequently / occasionally / once in a lifetime / never).
   b) i) If it still floods, say why you think it should *either* be allowed to continue to flood *or* be prevented from flooding.
      ii) If attempts have been made to prevent it from flooding, describe these attempts and say how successful you think they have been.

What are the main processes that produce coastal landforms?

EROSION

The wearing away of the land by material carried by waves and the removal of loose material (boulders, rock and sand)

Processes

1. When beach material is thrown against a cliff by large waves (**abrasion**).

2. When waves cause rocks and boulders on the beach to bump into each other, causing them to break into smaller pieces (**attrition**).

3. When certain rocks in cliffs are dissolved by salt and other acids in seawater (**solution** or **corrosion**).

4. When the sheer force of the waves hits a cliff (**hydraulic action**).

TRANSPORTATION

The picking up and movement of beach material by waves and off-shore currents

Processes

1. Waves move some beach material up and down the beach.

2. Off-shore currents can move material along the beach (**longshore drift**).

A

Land

Beach

Sea

A   Breaking waves carry material up the beach at an angle.

B   Backwash returns material straight down the beach.

Beach material moves in this direction

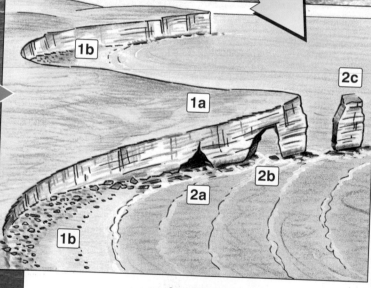

B

Landforms

1. Headlands and bays (diagram **D**, photo **E** on page 14; *Connections 14*).

2. Caves, arches and stacks (*Connections 14*).

Activities

1 a) What is the difference between erosion, transportation and deposition?
   b) Briefly describe the processes by which waves may erode the land.
   c) Briefly describe the processes by which waves and off-shore currents may transport material.
   d) Under what conditions may waves and off-shore currents deposit material?

2 Make a larger copy of map **C**, which shows part of the Yorkshire coast. Use information on these two pages and *Connections* 14–15 to answer the following.
   a) Label an area where each of:
      i) erosion
      ii) transportation and
      iii) deposition is most likely to occur.
   b) What coastal landforms are likely to be found at:
      i) Flamborough Head and
      ii) Spurn Head?
   c) Describe the coastal process between Flamborough Head and Spurn Head.

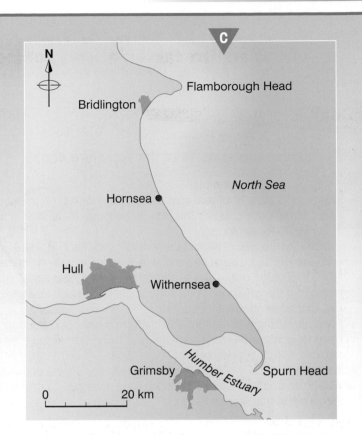

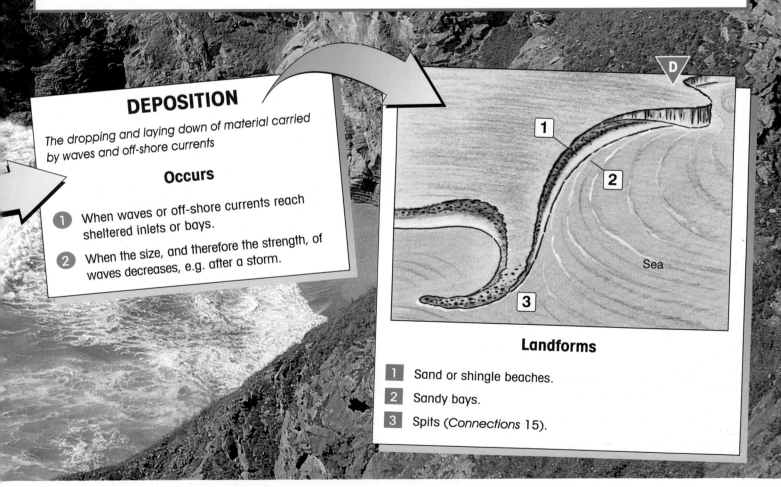

DEPOSITION

The dropping and laying down of material carried by waves and off-shore currents

Occurs

1 When waves or off-shore currents reach sheltered inlets or bays.

2 When the size, and therefore the strength, of waves decreases, e.g. after a storm.

Landforms

1 Sand or shingle beaches.

2 Sandy bays.

3 Spits (*Connections* 15).

What are the causes, effects and human response to cliff collapse ...

Cliff collapse along parts of the Yorkshire coast

Causes

- Where cliffs consist of resistant rock, as at Flamborough Head, waves erode at the base causing the cliffs to become unstable and to collapse (diagram **A**).
- Where cliffs consist of much less resistant rock, as in Holderness, rain can wash loose material downhill where, together with the softer material at the foot of the cliff, it can be rapidly removed by the waves (photo **B** – notice that the cliff made up of softer material is much less steep than that formed in resistant rock).
- Sand and shingle at the foot of cliffs form a natural protection. If this material is removed, as it sometimes is by human activity, then erosion and cliff retreat accelerates.
- Buildings built on cliff-tops (e.g. hotels with sea views) add weight which can contribute to cliff collapse (one hotel near Scarborough was destroyed in this way in 1993).

Effects of cliff collapse

The Holderness coastline is being worn back by an average of 2 metres a year. It is now some 3 km further west than it was in Roman times, and some 50 villages mentioned in the Domesday Book of 1086 have been lost to the sea (*Connections* 15 map **D**). Villages, campsites and farms, situated in places that a few years ago were thought to be safe, are now being abandoned and lost (photo **C**).

Human response

The towns of Hornsea and Withernsea have been protected by building concrete sea-walls. These walls are often curved towards the top to divert the force of the waves back out to sea (photo **D**). Elsewhere along the coast, wooden groynes have been built (photo **E**) and concrete rip-rap added (photo **F**), to try to reduce the power of the waves.

How have human responses caused problems?

The protection of one part of the coastline often only increases the problem of erosion elsewhere. Sea defences are very costly to construct and maintain, and people argue about who should pay for them. While those who are at risk from cliff collapse want their property protected, others feel that nature should be allowed to run its natural course. Many people also consider that the defences are unsightly.

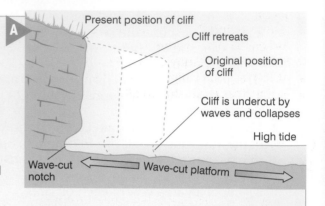

A

Present position of cliff
Cliff retreats
Original position of cliff
Cliff is undercut by waves and collapses
High tide
Wave-cut notch
Wave-cut platform

B

C

F

D

E

... and coastal flooding?

Coastal flooding

Causes
- Land behind the coastline is flat and low-lying (or, in the case of the Netherlands, even below sea-level).
- Severe storms may create exceptionally high waves.
- At times of very high tides, the sea can flood the land.
- Rising sea-levels due to global warming are an increasing threat.

Case Study

Effects of the 1990 coastal flood at Towyn, North Wales

The inhabitants of Towyn, seemingly protected by a sea-wall, were unprepared for the events of August 1990 (map **G**). A severe storm, accompanied by northerly winds of up to 140 km/hour, huge waves and a series of high tides, caused a 200-metre break in the sea-wall (photo **H**). Within a short time, most of the town was flooded to a depth of over 1 metre, and the sea had spread up to 8 km inland. More than 2,000 people were made homeless, with many of the elderly and young having to be rescued by boat, and one-quarter of the families had no house insurance. Huge lorries brought boulders from a local quarry to try to repair the gap in the sea-wall, but progress was hindered by further storms. A week later high tides were still causing flooding, and emergency services were still trying to repair the wall, and to restore supplies of gas, electricity and water.

How can a repeat flooding of Towyn be prevented? Those at greatest risk wanted a larger and stronger sea-wall to be built (photo **I**), but others felt it was no use trying to fight nature, especially as sea-walls are expensive and unsightly. Other suggestions included moving people and industry away from flood-prone areas (some inhabitants did move out), making greater attempts to control global warming, and predicting that a similar event would not occur again in their lifetime.

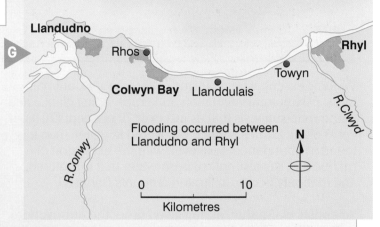

Activities

1. What causes:
   a) cliffs to collapse and retreat
   b) coastal flooding?

2. Divide your geography set into four groups. After time for discussion:
   a) Group 1 should explain why they are in favour of protecting cliffs from erosion and retreat.
   b) Group 2 should say why they would allow cliffs to erode and retreat.
   c) Group 3 should give reasons why they think places should be protected from coastal flooding.
   d) Group 4 should say why they would allow coastal flooding to continue.

What are the components and links in the water cycle?

97.2%	occurs in seas and oceans but, as it is salty, it is only readily available to marine life	**A**
2.1%	is water stored on the Earth's surface as ice and snow (mainly in the ice-caps of Antarctica and Greenland)	
0.7%	is fresh water: 0.6% is water stored in rivers and lakes, 0.1% is water stored underground in soil and rocks, and 0.001% is stored as water vapour (a gas) in the atmosphere	

Water is essential for all forms of life – people, animals, birds, fish, natural vegetation and crops. A first glance at a world map suggests that as just over 70 per cent (70.9 per cent) of the Earth's surface is covered in water, then it is found in abundance. However, with the exception of marine life, it is a supply of fresh water that is required, and that only occurs in limited amounts (table **A**).

Scientists claim that, at any given time, the atmosphere only holds sufficient water vapour to provide the Earth with 10 days of rain. This means that this small amount of water vapour has to be constantly recycled between the oceans, atmosphere and land (*Foundations* 36 diagram **A**). It is this recycling of water that is known as the **hydrological**, or **water**, **cycle**. As diagram **B** shows, the hydrological cycle consists of:

- four **components**, i.e. evaporation, condensation, precipitation and run-off
- four **linkages**, i.e. movements (or flows) between the components.

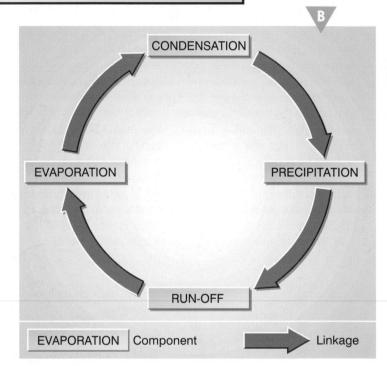

In reality the water cycle is more complicated than this (diagram **C**). For example:

- Evaporation should really be referred to as **evapotranspiration** as it includes evaporation directly from water surfaces (rivers, lakes) as well as transpiration (water loss) from plants.
- Precipitation includes the deposition of water on the Earth's surface both in a liquid form (rain, drizzle) and as a solid (snow, hail).
- Run-off can either be over the Earth's surface (in rivers), or through the soil (as throughflow), or at deeper levels (as groundwater).

Water within the cycle can also be **stored** in different forms and in various places. Storage includes:

- as water (a liquid) within oceans and seas
- as vapour (a gas) in the atmosphere
- as snow and ice (a solid) in mountainous areas or places nearer the Poles

- as water (a liquid) in lakes or swamps on the Earth's surface
- as water (a liquid) within rocks and the soil.

It should also be noted that the water cycle is not always continuous and it can, from time to time, experience interruptions. Such interruptions may occur:

- during very cold spells in winter (or during an ice age) when water is stored as ice and snow and run-off is greatly reduced
- during times of drought when there is also reduced run-off
- following times of heavy rainfall when excessive run-off creates floods
- as a result of human activity, e.g. building dams (and so reducing run-off) or polluting freshwater supplies.

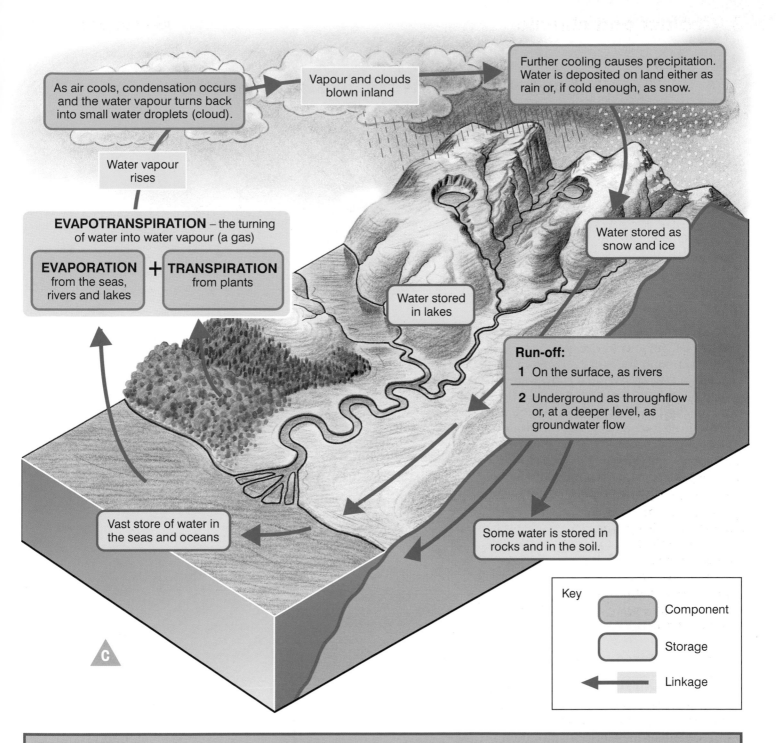

As air cools, condensation occurs and the water vapour turns back into small water droplets (cloud).

Vapour and clouds blown inland

Further cooling causes precipitation. Water is deposited on land either as rain or, if cold enough, as snow.

Water vapour rises

EVAPOTRANSPIRATION – the turning of water into water vapour (a gas)

EVAPORATION from the seas, rivers and lakes **+** **TRANSPIRATION** from plants

Water stored as snow and ice

Water stored in lakes

Run-off:

1 On the surface, as rivers

2 Underground as throughflow or, at a deeper level, as groundwater flow

Vast store of water in the seas and oceans

Some water is stored in rocks and in the soil.

Key

Component

Storage

Linkage

C

Activities

1 a) Name the four components in the water cycle.
   b) With reference to *Foundations* 37, give a definition for each of the four components.
   c) Describe how the four components within the water cycle are linked.

2 Within the water cycle:
   a) Name three forms in which water can be found.
   b) Name four ways in which water (in any form) may be stored.

3 Diagram **D** shows an interruption to the water cycle. Describe two ways in which the water cycle can be interrupted.

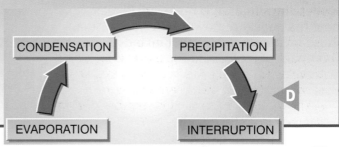

CONDENSATION

PRECIPITATION

EVAPORATION

INTERRUPTION

D

Why do temperatures vary from place to place?

Temperatures vary from place to place and at different times of the year due to one, or more, of the reasons shown on these two pages (maps **A** and **B**).

Latitude

Places that are nearer the Equator are much warmer than places nearer to the Poles (compare places A and B on both maps). This is for two reasons (diagram **C**).

1 The curvature of the Earth and the angle of the sun in the sky
At the Equator the sun is always at a high angle in the sky. When it is overhead it actually shines vertically downwards. This means that its heat is concentrated on a small area and, as a result, the ground heats up very rapidly. Going towards the Poles, the sun's angle decreases. As the sun's heat now has a greater area to warm up, then temperatures are lower.

2 The layer of atmosphere that surrounds the Earth
The atmosphere contains dust and other solid particles which can absorb heat coming from the sun. As the sun's rays pass more directly through the atmosphere at the Equator than at the Poles, then less heat is lost at the Equator.

Distance from the sea

As liquids (the sea) are less dense than solids (the land), they take much longer to warm up but, once warmed, they then retain their heat much longer (*Interactions* 4 diagram **A**). This means that in summer, places near the sea are cooler than places located towards the centre of continents (compare places C and D on map **B**). In winter, the situation is reversed. Places near the coast are now much warmer than those located much further inland (compare places C and D on map **A**).

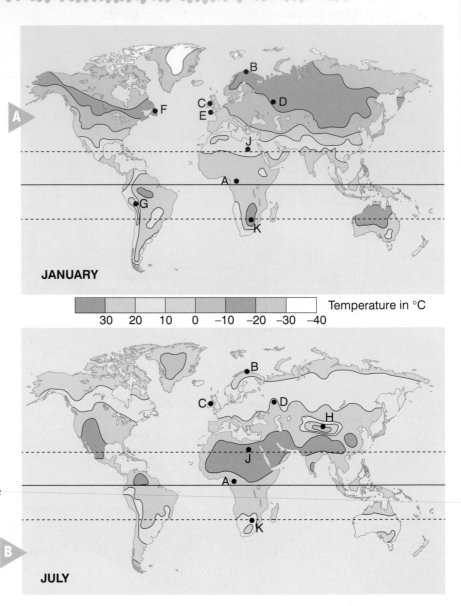

JANUARY

Temperature in °C

| 30 | 20 | 10 | 0 | −10 | −20 | −30 | −40 |

JULY

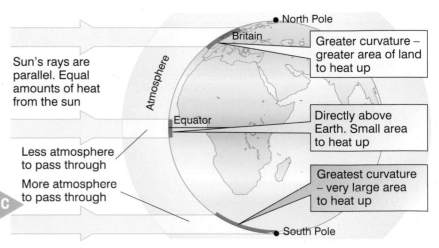

Sun's rays are parallel. Equal amounts of heat from the sun

Less atmosphere to pass through

More atmosphere to pass through

North Pole

Britain

Greater curvature – greater area of land to heat up

Equator

Directly above Earth. Small area to heat up

Greatest curvature – very large area to heat up

South Pole

Atmosphere

Prevailing winds

The prevailing wind is the direction from which the wind is most likely to come, i.e. from the south-west in Britain. If it blows over a warm surface (the land in summer or the sea in winter) it will raise temperatures. If it blows over a cooler surface (the land in winter or the sea in summer) it will lower temperatures (*Interactions* 5 diagram **D**).

Ocean currents

Coastal areas are affected by ocean currents (map **D**). These may either raise temperatures (i.e. a warm current such as the North Atlantic Drift – place E on map **A**) or lower temperatures (i.e. a cold current such as the Labrador Current – place F on map **A**).

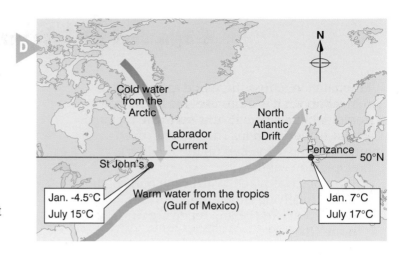

Altitude (height of the land)

Temperature decreases, on average, by 1°C for every 100 metres in height (diagram **E**). Notice the effect of the Andes (place G on map **A**) and the Himalayas (place H on map **B**) on temperatures.

Seasons

Maps **A** and **B** show how changes in the seasons affect world temperatures. Notice the difference between places J and K on map **A** (which is winter in the northern hemisphere and summer in the southern hemisphere) and map **B** (where it is now summer in the northern hemisphere and winter in the southern hemisphere).

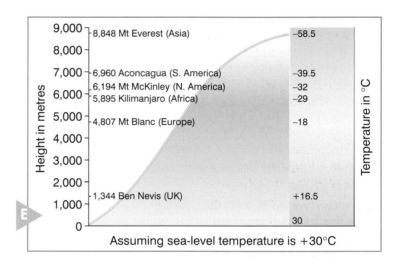

Activities

1 Make a copy of table **F**. Complete it by giving:
   a) differences in temperature by using maps **A** and **B**
   b) reasons for the differences in temperature.

2 a) How do each of the following factors affect temperatures?
   - latitude
   - prevailing winds
   - altitude
   - distance from the sea
   - ocean currents
   - seasons

   b) Which of the factors listed in part **a)** do you think affect temperatures in the British Isles?

Places		Difference in temperature (to nearest 10°C)	Main reason for difference
A and B	in January		
	in July		
C and D	in January		
	in July		
E and F	in January		
A and G	in January		
D and H	in July		
J and K	in January		
	in July		

29

Why does rainfall vary from place to place?

Precipitation across the world usually falls as rain, although it is more likely to be snow in colder latitudes (Arctic and Antarctic regions) and at higher altitudes (mountains, even including those located on the Equator). Precipitation varies:

- from place to place, with some parts of the world receiving large amounts (over 3,000 mm a year) and others receiving virtually none (map **A**)
- from season to season, with some places receiving rain throughout the year (equatorial areas, the UK) and others at only certain times (Mediterranean in winter, tropical interiors in summer)
- from year to year, with most places having variable amounts (e.g. southern Britain had a drought in 1995 and was very wet in 1998)
- in type, i.e. relief, convectional and frontal rainfall (*Foundations* 22–23).

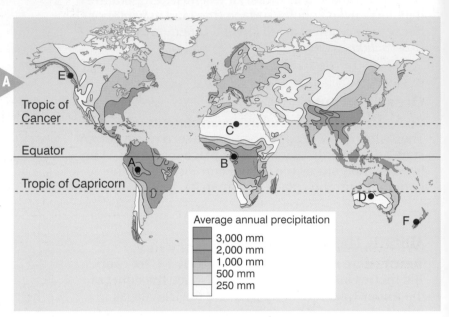

Why does it rain?

We have already seen that rainfall, or precipitation, forms part of the water cycle (diagram **C** page 27). It occurs when warm air causes water on the ground, in the sea and from vegetation, to evaporate – **evaporation** being the process by which water (a liquid) is turned into water vapour (a gas). If the warm, moist air is **forced** to rise, then it will cool (remember, temperature decreases with height – see page 29). If the air cools sufficiently it will reach dew point (diagram **B**). **Dew point** is the temperature at which air becomes saturated with water vapour. If the air continues to rise and to cool, then condensation occurs – **condensation** is the process by which water vapour (a gas) turns back into water droplets (a liquid) or, if the temperature is below 0°C, into snow (a solid) – and clouds will form. Further cooling and condensation will produce precipitation.

There are three main types of rainfall – **convectional**, **relief** and **frontal** (*Foundations* 22–23). In all three cases, the process by which rain forms is the same (diagram **B**). The only difference between them is what **forces** the warm, moist air to rise in the first place (figure **C**).

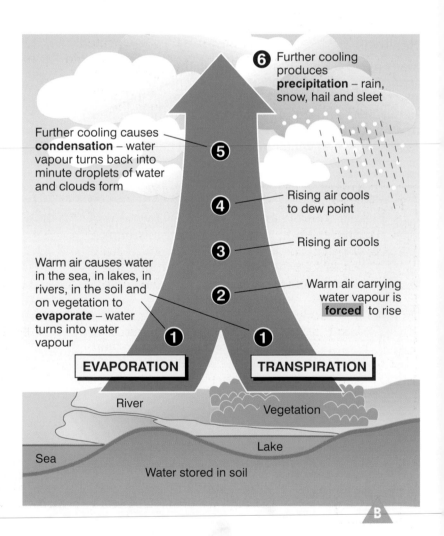

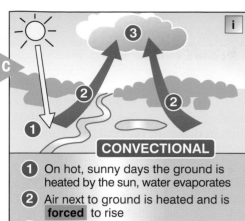

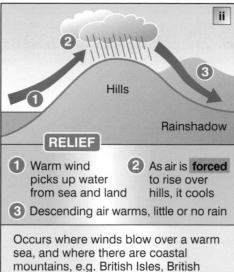

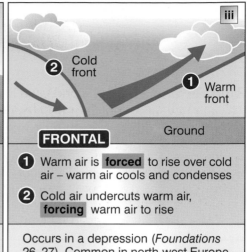

CONVECTIONAL i

1 On hot, sunny days the ground is heated by the sun, water evaporates

2 Air next to ground is heated and is **forced** to rise

3 Rising air cools and condenses

Occurs most afternoons near to the Equator. May occur in southern Britain after several hot days in summer.

RELIEF ii

1 Warm wind picks up water from sea and land

2 As air is **forced** to rise over hills, it cools

3 Descending air warms, little or no rain

Occurs where winds blow over a warm sea, and where there are coastal mountains, e.g. British Isles, British Columbia, South Island of New Zealand

FRONTAL iii

1 Warm air is **forced** to rise over cold air – warm air cools and condenses

2 Cold air undercuts warm air, **forcing** warm air to rise

Occurs in a depression (*Foundations* 26–27). Common in north-west Europe, British Columbia and South Island of New Zealand.

Why do some places receive very little rainfall?

There are two main reasons why some parts of the world receive very little rainfall (map **A**).

- Some places are protected from winds blowing from the sea by high mountains. Such places are said to lie in a **rainshadow** (diagram **C** ii).
- Other places are very dry because they are located where the air high above them is relatively cold. Cold air sinks (diagram **D**). As the cold air sinks, it warms up and is able to pick up moisture and there is no condensation. Such places, which include the Sahara, are desert.

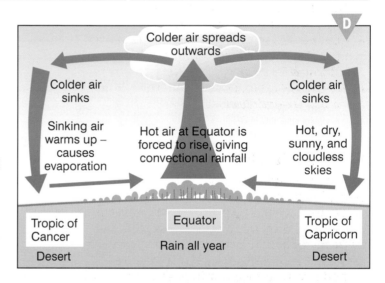

Activities

1 With reference to map **A**:
   a) Why do places A and B have high rainfall totals throughout the year?
   b) Why do places C and D receive very little rainfall?
   c) Why do places on the coast, such as at E and F, receive high annual rainfall totals?

2 a) Complete diagram **E** by putting the following terms associated with the rainmaking process into their correct order:

- Clouds form
- Dew point
- Precipitation
- Rising air cools
- Transpiration
- Condensation
- Evaporation
- Rain
- Snow
- Warm, moist air forced to rise

   b) The only difference in the rainmaking process (which you illustrated in **a**)) for convectional, relief and frontal rainfall, is the **cause** of the warm, moist air being forced to rise. Explain, for each of the three types, why the air is forced to rise.

Why do weather and climate vary over the British Isles?

Weather and climate

Weather describes the short-term state of the atmosphere which may last for several hours or perhaps for a few days. It includes temperature, sunshine, precipitation, cloud cover and wind. Although most people are only interested in, and affected by, weather in their local area (i.e. within a few kilometres), the daily weather map on TV or in a newspaper reminds us that weather events are global, e.g. there are hurricanes, heat waves and floods in different parts of the world.

Climate is much longer-term and describes the average conditions over a period of years. It gives the expected, rather than the actual, conditions for a place and is often applied to sizeable parts of the Earth, e.g. the equatorial or Mediterranean climate.

Activities

1 Read the forecast in figure **A**. Copy and complete the table underneath by putting those phrases in the forecast that refer to 'weather' in the first column and those that refer to 'climate' in the second column.

A

'Tomorrow will be very warm with temperatures reaching 27°C, which is several degrees warmer than the seasonal average. It will be sunny, although there is a slight risk of a thunderstorm in some parts which might break the drought.

So far this month, rainfall has been less than half what we would normally expect. Winds will remain gentle and from the south-east, although next week they are expected to return to their prevailing south-westerly direction.'

Weather	Climate

2 Map **B** (and *Foundations* 21 map **E**) shows how the British Isles may be divided into four climatic regions.
  a) Which of the four quarters has:
     i)   the highest temperature in January (winter)
     ii) the lowest temperature in January
     iii) the highest temperature in July (summer)
     iv) the lowest temperature in July
     v)   the most rainfall in a year
     vi) the least rainfall in a year?
  b) Why is western Britain warmer than eastern Britain in winter? (See page 29, and *Foundations* 20 map **A**.)
  c) Why is southern Britain warmer than northern Britain in summer? (See page 28, and *Foundations* 20 map **B**.)
  d) Why does western Britain receive more rainfall than eastern Britain? (See page 31, and *Foundations* 21 map **D**.)

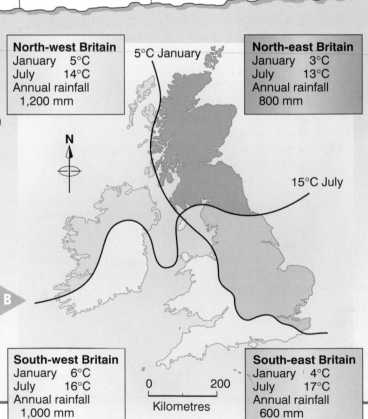

North-west Britain
January   5°C
July   14°C
Annual rainfall
  1,200 mm

5°C January

North-east Britain
January   3°C
July   13°C
Annual rainfall
  800 mm

N

15°C July

South-west Britain
January   6°C
July   16°C
Annual rainfall
  1,000 mm

0   200
Kilometres

South-east Britain
January   4°C
July   17°C
Annual rainfall
  600 mm

B

Enquiry

a) Keep a record of the weather for a month

Decide, as a class, what weather data you need to collect (*Foundations* 16–17) and then how you will collect the data, e.g.

   i)   school logging weather station (photo **C**)

   ii) school manual weather station

   iii) use of TV and/or the local newspaper.

b) How to record the weather data

The class should, if possible, use ICT to record the data. As a group, use a computer to create a spreadsheet to record the daily weather for a month (figure **D**). Draw up a rota so that all members of the class are given the opportunity to record onto the spreadsheet. A datalogging weather station stores the data continuously, making it possible to download the information for weekends and holidays.

A datalogging weather station

Month	Date	Temperature	Precipitation	Wind speed	Wind direction	Cloud
June	1					
	2					
	3					
	4					
	5					

c) Additional/alternative data to collect

During the period that the class is recording the weather, a range of other information could also be collected. If your school has a link to the Internet, it is possible to download and print out weather satellite images from either of the two websites shown in figure **E** i and ii. If not, you could either record on video a sequence of TV weather forecasts or collect a series of forecasts from a national or local newspaper (figure **E** iii).

d) How to present the data

At the end of the recording period the class needs to divide into groups. Each group should be allocated one element of the weather, for which data was collected, and given a copy of the spreadsheet. They should then use the spreadsheet to create and print out a chart for their given weather element.

e) Analysing the data and producing a weather report

   i)   Use all the weather charts, and any other information collected, to write a weather report.

   ii) Read about depressions (*Foundations* 26–27) and anticyclones (*Foundations* 24–25). Compare the charts which your class produced for the different weather elements that were recorded, and see if there are any patterns suggesting that weather is influenced by depressions and/or anticyclones. Any sequence of satellite images or weather forecasts that you kept will also help with this.

   iii) You could wordprocess your report and insert an example of one of the charts from the spreadsheet, before printing. Remember to give your report a title, and to save your processed report onto a floppy disc.

Netscape – [Welcome to Netscape]
File Edit View Go Bookmarks Options Directory Window Help

http://www.meto.gov.uk

Met Office homepage gives minute information about weather, including regional forecasts and satellite images updated every 6 hours

(i)

Netscape – [Welcome to Netscape]
File Edit View Go Bookmarks Options Directory Window Help

http://www.bbc.co.uk/weather/

BBC weather page. Latest forecast of the UK's weather, including latest satellite image

(ii)

UK TOMORROW

Strong northerly winds will bring snow showers to the far north of Scotland and the northern isles. Further south the snow will turn to rain, with possibly some thunder in the west. The far south, by contrast, can expect some clear periods with sunshine.

(iii)

Why do weather and climate vary around the world?

There are great variations in weather over the Earth's surface. This gives rise to several specific climatic types, four of which are shown on figure **A**.

Climate graphs

The four climate graphs, all for places on or north of the Equator, show considerable differences (Activity 1) between:

- January/winter/minimum temperatures
- July/summer/maximum temperatures
- annual range in temperature (the difference between the warmest and the coldest month, i.e. the maximum temperature minus the minimum temperature)
- the total annual amount of rainfall
- the seasonal distribution of rainfall.

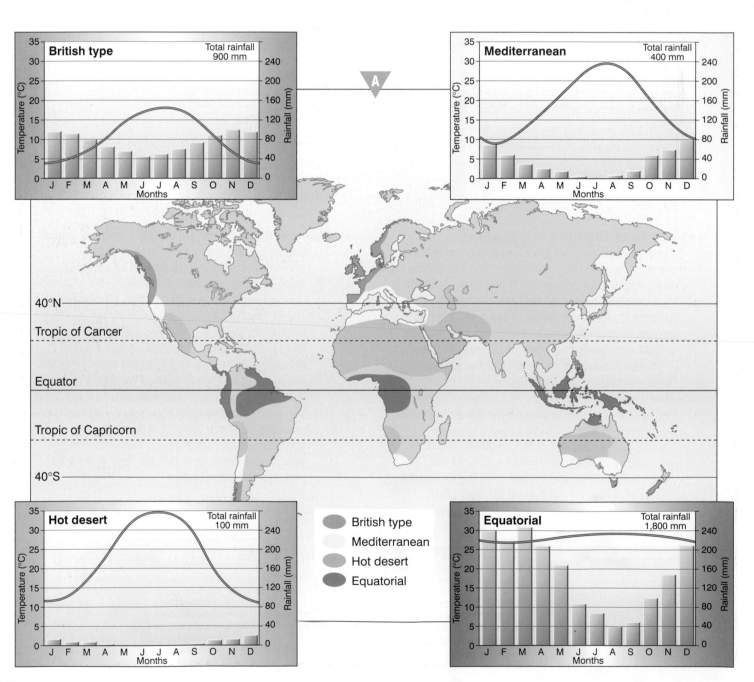

Location map

Figure **A** also shows the location of the four climatic types. (If you find this rather complex to understand, you should refer back to the four individual maps in *Interactions* 6, 9, 13 and 17). If you look closely you will see that each climate type does not appear at random, but there is a **pattern**. Geographers need to be able to:

- identify and describe patterns (Activity 2)
- analyse (i.e. give reasons for) such patterns (Activity 3).

Activities

1 a) With reference to the four graphs in figure **A**, copy and complete table **B**.

b) With reference to your completed table **B**, which climatic type has:
   i) the highest temperature in July
   ii) the lowest temperature in July
   iii) the highest temperature in January
   iv) the lowest temperature in January
   v) the greatest range in temperature
   vi) the lowest range in temperature
   vii) the most rainfall during a year
   viii) the least rainfall during a year
   ix) most rain in winter and little rain in summer
   x) rain falling throughout the year (two types of climate)?

c) For each type of climate, write:
   i) one sentence to summarise its temperature
   ii) one sentence to summarise its rainfall.
   (If you struggle with this question, refer back to each of the individual climate graphs in *Interactions* 6, 8, 12 and 16.)

2 With reference to the map in figure **A**:
   a) Describe the location of each of the four types of climate. Your description might be related to whether the climate is on the coast or inland; on the east or the west coast; inside or outside the tropics (i.e. related to latitude).

	British type	Mediterranean	Hot desert	Equatorial
July temperature °C				
January temperature °C				
Annual temp. range °C				
Annual rainfall mm				
Seasonal distribution of rainfall				

B

b) Copy and complete table **C** by naming for each type at least three areas (or three countries) in different continents.
When you have completed parts **a)** and **b)** – and only then – you could check your answers with text and figures in *Interactions* 6, 9, 13 and 17.

3 Give reasons for (analyse) the location of each of the four types of climate. Table **D** is a checklist, based on pages 28–31, intended to help you with your answers.
(If you can answer this question then you really have understood weather and climate.)

Location examples	1	2	3
British type			
Mediterranean			
Hot desert			
Equatorial			

C

Temperature	Rainfall
latitude	• Rising air: convectional relief frontal
distance from the sea	
prevailing winds	
ocean currents	
altitude	• Descending air: dry
seasons	

D

4 Ecosystems

What are the main components of an ecosystem?

What is an ecosystem?

An **ecosystem** is a natural system which links together the living and the non-living environment (table **A**). In it the lives of plants and animals are closely linked to each other and to the climate, soil and vegetation of the area in which they grow or live (diagram **B**).

Ecosystems can vary enormously in scale:
- Small, or microscale, e.g. under a leaf or a stone
- Medium scale, e.g. a woodland, a sand-dune, a saltmarsh
- Large, or global scale, e.g. tropical rainforest (pages 38–39), tropical grassland (pages 40–41).

Ecosystems depend upon two basic processes.

1 A continuous flow of energy

The main source of energy in any ecosystem is sunlight. Sunlight is taken in by the green leaves of plants. It is then converted, by a process known as **photosynthesis**, into a form of energy which can pass through the ecosystem in the **food chain** (diagram **C**). The food chain is when animals (or birds and fish) either eat green plants directly, or consume other animals (or birds and fish) which have previously eaten green plants.

Non-living environment	Living environment	A
Solar energy Water Air (O_2, CO_2) Rocks and soil	Flora (plants) Fauna (animals and decomposers)	

Human activity has increasingly interrupted, and even destroyed, many ecosystems

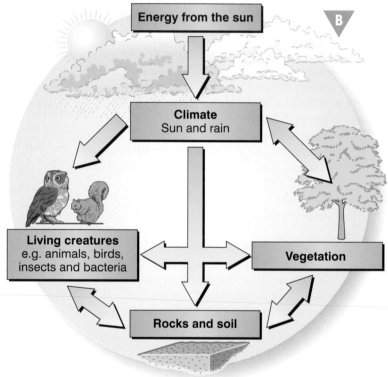

B

Energy from the sun

Climate — Sun and rain

Living creatures e.g. animals, birds, insects and bacteria

Vegetation

Rocks and soil

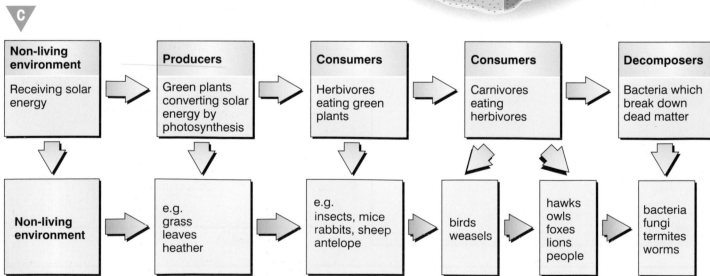

C

Non-living environment	Producers	Consumers	Consumers	Decomposers
Receiving solar energy	Green plants converting solar energy by photosynthesis	Herbivores eating green plants	Carnivores eating herbivores	Bacteria which break down dead matter
Non-living environment	e.g. grass leaves heather	e.g. insects, mice rabbits, sheep antelope	birds weasels — hawks owls foxes lions people	bacteria fungi termites worms

2 The recycling of nutrients

Nutrients include minerals such as carbon, nitrogen, phosphorus and potassium which are essential for plant growth. Nutrients are found in the soil and result from the weathering of underlying rock (page 15). In the nutrient cycle (diagram **D**), nutrients and water are taken up from the soil by the roots of plants and trees. They are later returned to the soil either when the plant sheds its leaves or when the vegetation dies and decomposes.

Animal life also needs nutrients. It obtains them through the food chain by eating either plants or animal life which has previously eaten plants. Animal life returns nutrients to the soil either through its excreta, or, as with vegetation, when it too dies and decomposes.

The nutrient cycle is often broken, usually with serious consequences, by human activities such as farming and deforestation.

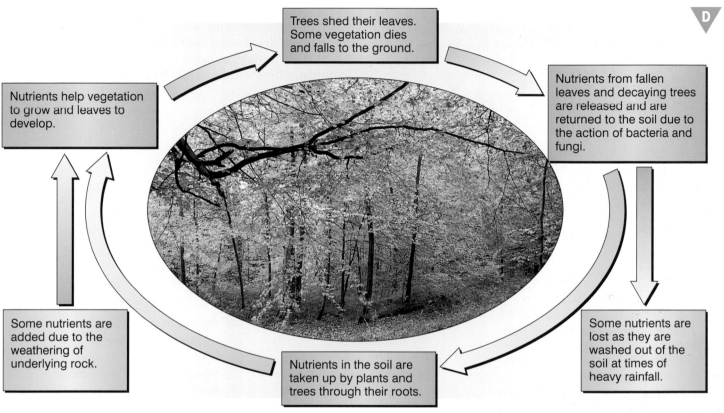

D

Trees shed their leaves. Some vegetation dies and falls to the ground.

Nutrients from fallen leaves and decaying trees are released and are returned to the soil due to the action of bacteria and fungi.

Nutrients help vegetation to grow and leaves to develop.

Some nutrients are added due to the weathering of underlying rock.

Nutrients in the soil are taken up by plants and trees through their roots.

Some nutrients are lost as they are washed out of the soil at times of heavy rainfall.

Activities

1 a) What is an ecosystem?
   b) What is the difference between the 'living' and the 'non-living' environment?
   c) What is the main source of energy in an ecosystem?
   d) How is energy passed through an ecosystem?

2 On a copy of diagram **E**, place each of the following labels in the appropriate place.

- air, water, rocks and soil
- bacteria and fungi
- carnivores
- consumers
- consumers
- decomposers
- deer and rabbits
- grass and leaves
- grass eaters
- green plants
- herbivores
- lions and owls
- meat eaters
- non-living environment
- photosynthesis
- producers
- sun's energy

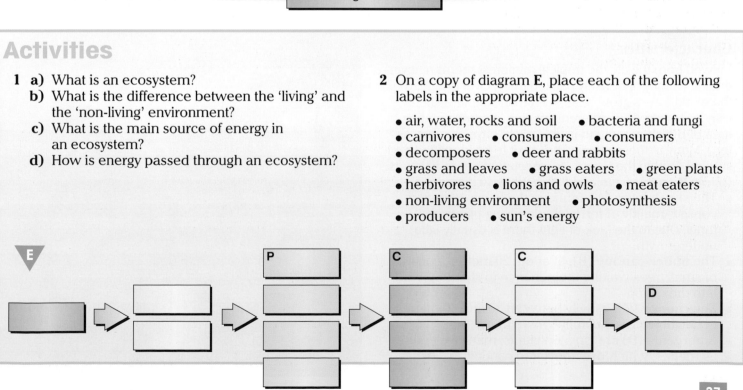

E

P   C   C   D

Which physical and human processes influence the tropical rainforests?

Distribution

The tropical rainforest forms one of the world's largest ecosystems. Normally, it is associated with the equatorial climate (figure **A** on page 34). This climate, with its high rainfall totals and constantly high temperatures, is found mainly between 5° North and 5° South of the Equator. It is these forests that are described on these two pages.

However, if you look at a world vegetation map, such as map **A** or in an atlas, you will notice that the tropical rainforest has a much wider distribution:

- on tropical east coasts of continents where prevailing winds from the sea bring large amounts of rainfall for most of the year
- in parts of South-east Asia where heavy summer monsoon rains (*Connections* 26) can bring enough moisture in several months to support forest.

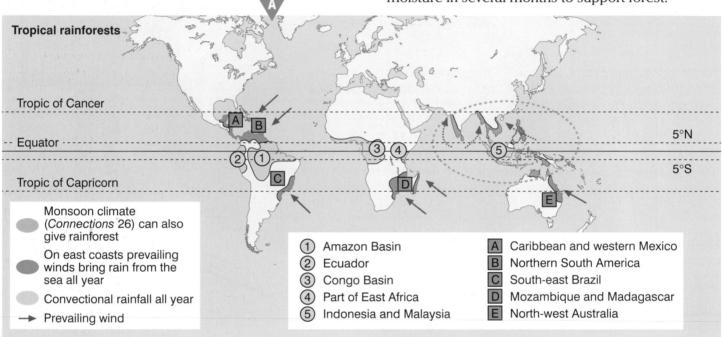

Tropical rainforests

Tropic of Cancer

Equator

Tropic of Capricorn

5°N

5°S

Monsoon climate (*Connections* 26) can also give rainforest

On east coasts prevailing winds bring rain from the sea all year

Convectional rainfall all year

→ Prevailing wind

1. Amazon Basin
2. Ecuador
3. Congo Basin
4. Part of East Africa
5. Indonesia and Malaysia

A. Caribbean and western Mexico
B. Northern South America
C. South-east Brazil
D. Mozambique and Madagascar
E. North-west Australia

Characteristics

Viewed from the air, the tropical rainforest seems a never-ending canopy of densely packed trees. Over one-third of the world's trees grow here. Within one hectare, there may be hundreds of different species (a corresponding area of British woodland is unlikely to have as many as ten). Many of these species have yet to be identified and studied. Within the forest, the vegetation grows in layers (photo **B** on this page and *Interactions* 10 diagram **A**).

- The **shrub layer** (A), found in the lower 10 metres, consists mainly of ferns, shade-loving plants and fungi. Due to the lack of light there is usually little undergrowth.
- The **under-canopy** (B), at about 20 metres, consists of small trees waiting their chance to shoot upwards into the canopy.
- The **canopy** (C), usually between 30 and 40 metres in height, consists of fully-grown trees.
- **Emergents** (D) are isolated giants, many exceeding 50 metres, which rise above the canopy.

Relationship between climate and vegetation

Description	Reasons
Forest has an evergreen appearance as trees can shed leaves at any time	Continuous growing season
Trees grow very rapidly	Hot and wet throughout the year
Trees grow very tall	
Tallest trees are straight and branchless in their lower parts	To try to reach sunlight
Lianas (rope-like vines – photo **C**) climb up tree trunks	
Very little undergrowth except near to rivers	Sunlight unable to penetrate the canopy
Leaves have drip tips (*Interactions* 10)	To shed water quickly after heavy afternoon thunderstorms

Relationship between soil and vegetation

The hot, wet climate is ideal for the rapid decay of vegetation. Decomposers, such as fungi and termites, cause the breakdown of dead plants and leaves. As the vegetation rots and decays, large amounts of nutrients are released into the soil ready to be taken up again by living plants in the nutrient cycle (diagram **D** page 37). Soils are deep, due to rapid chemical weathering of the underlying rock (page 15). However, tree roots are shallow as most of the nutrients are found near to the surface and trees have had to develop huge buttress roots for support (photo **E**). The soil is usually red in colour.

Influence of human activity on vegetation

Indians living in the rainforest have always cleared small areas of land on which to build their houses and grow their crops. However, they lived in harmony with the environment, moving on before they had totally destroyed the soil of an area (*Places* 26). More recently, however, large logging, cattle-ranching and mining companies have cleared huge areas of forest without any thought for the soil (page 88). The fragile forest ecosystem is destroyed because:

- once the forest is cleared then, without the addition of leaves and decaying vegetation, the nutrient cycle is broken and the soil soon becomes infertile
- the soil, without a vegetation cover to protect it from the heavy rain, can easily be eroded and washed away (soil erosion)
- the rain also removes any remaining nutrients from the topsoil by washing them downwards in a process known as **leaching**.

Rainforest soils can become useless within four or five years.

Activities

1 a) Write a short paragraph describing the general appearance of the tropical rainforest.
   b) How have the trees in the tropical rainforest adapted to the hot, wet climate?
   c) Why is the relationship between soils and vegetation so important in the tropical rainforest?

2 Diagram **F** shows what can happen when the rainforest is cleared for human activity. Explain how:
   a) the nutrient cycle is broken
   b) the soil soon becomes infertile.

Which physical and human processes influence the tropical grasslands?

Distribution

The tropical savanna grasslands form one of the world's largest ecosystems. It is the type of vegetation associated with the tropical continental climate. This climate, which is very warm throughout the year, is characterised by its summer rainfall and winter drought (graph **A**). It is located in the centre of continents approximately between latitudes 5° and 20° North and South of the Equator (map **B**). It is also found straddling the Equator in Africa on the higher land of the East African Plateau (Kenya and Tanzania).

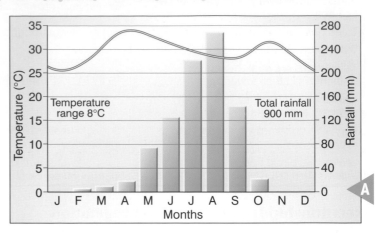

Temperature range 8°C

Total rainfall 900 mm

A

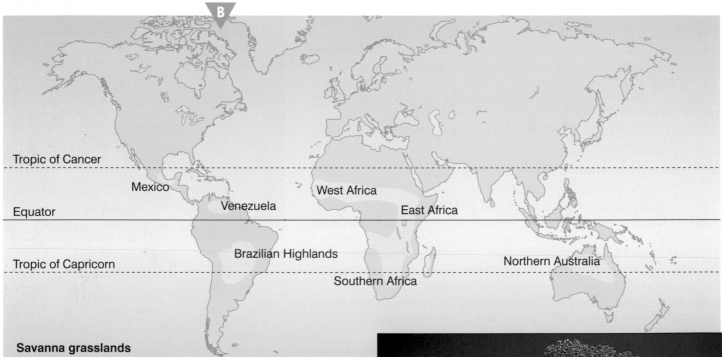

Tropic of Cancer

Mexico

West Africa

Equator

Venezuela

East Africa

Brazilian Highlands

Tropic of Capricorn

Northern Australia

Southern Africa

Savanna grasslands

B

Characteristics

The true savanna grassland tends to be tussocks of grass with scattered trees. On the joint plain of the Maasai Mara (south-west Kenya) and the Serengeti (north-west Tanzania), the grassland seems to stretch for ever. Two of the more characteristic trees are the acacias, with their flat tops and Y-shaped trunks, and the baobab, or 'upside-down tree' (photo **C**). Where the savanna grasslands gradually merge with the tropical rainforest (on their equatorial side) the number of trees increases considerably. Where they merge with the hot desert (on the tropical side) the vegetation increasingly turns to scattered clumps of grass and drought-resistant bushes.

C

Relationship between climate and vegetation

Description	Reasons
In summer, the grasses grow very quickly, reaching a height of 3 or 4 metres (photo **E**).	Summers are very warm and wet
In winter, the grasses turn yellow, become straw-like and eventually die, leaving just their roots (photo **F**).	Winter drought
Many trees have long roots to tap underground water supplies.	
The baobab stores water in its trunk.	
Many trees have a thick bark.	To prevent transpiration (page 26)
Some plants have thorns as leaves, others have waxy leaves, some shed their leaves in winter.	
Trees like the baobab have a thick bark.	Protection against fires started by lightning

D

E

F

Relationship between soil and vegetation

During winter, as the grasses die, nutrients are returned to the soil (but not nearly in such large amounts as in the tropical rainforest). Water is also drawn upwards towards the surface – the process of **capillary action**. During early summer, before the grasses have grown sufficiently, the early rains can carry away the bare surface soil (soil erosion) and wash nutrients downwards – the process of **leaching**. The seasonal variation between capillary action and leaching produces a hard layer which impedes drainage and root penetration.

Influence of human activity on vegetation

The vegetation has been altered over time by fire – either started deliberately by farmers or naturally during thunderstorms. More recently, the grasslands have been changed as a result of rapid population growth, especially in Africa (*Places* 50–51). Trees and shrubs are being removed for fuelwood (*Connections* 56). Cropland is being overcultivated in an attempt to produce more food. The extension of towns and cultivated land means less space for animals which leads to overgrazing (*Interactions* 32). The collection of fuelwood, overcultivation and overgrazing all contribute to soil erosion and, in drier areas, **desertification**.

Activities

1 a) Write a short paragraph describing the general appearance of the savanna grasslands.
   b) How has the vegetation of the savanna grasslands adapted to the climate?
   c) What is the relationship between soils and vegetation in the savanna grasslands?

G
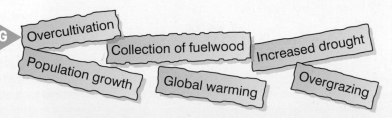

Overcultivation
Collection of fuelwood
Increased drought
Population growth
Global warming
Overgrazing

2 Diagram **G** gives some key words in the process of desertification. Write a short account, which you could give to the rest of your class, describing this process. You may have to research your answer from your school library.

5 Population

Why is the world's population unevenly distributed?

It was estimated that, during 1998, the population of the world passed the 6 billion mark. However, these 6,000,000,000 people are not spread out evenly across the Earth's surface. *Interactions* 84 map **A** is an extremely simplified map, with an equally simplified key, showing the location of those places considered to be 'crowded', those with 'few people' and those 'in between'.

Map **A** below shows (in more detail than in *Interactions* but still simplified in comparison with reality) the **density**, or degree of crowding, of the world's population.

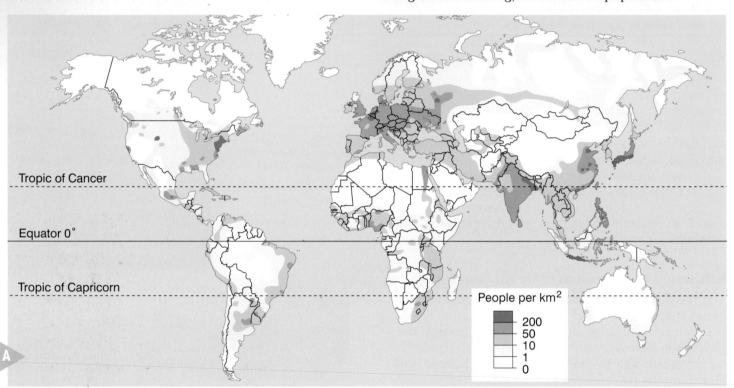

Tropic of Cancer

Equator 0°

Tropic of Capricorn

People per km²

- 200
- 50
- 10
- 1
- 0

A

Population density is the number of people living in a given area, usually a square kilometre (figure **B**). Places that are crowded and have a high population density are said to be **densely populated**. Places that only have a few people living there and have a low population density are said to be **sparsely populated**. Population density can be measured at a range of scales. Graphs **C** show differences between continents at the global scale, Activity **1** suggests differences between countries, while *Connections* 64 map **A** shows differences within a country (the UK). You could even extend this down to the county in which you live, and individual towns and cities within that county.

Population density $= \dfrac{\text{Total number of people living in an area}}{\text{Total area (km}^2)}$

1997

UK $\dfrac{58,306,000}{241,600} = 241$

England $\dfrac{49,089,000}{130,423} = 376$

Northumberland $\dfrac{307,400}{5,026} = 61$

Greater London $\dfrac{7,074,300}{1,578} = 4,482$

B

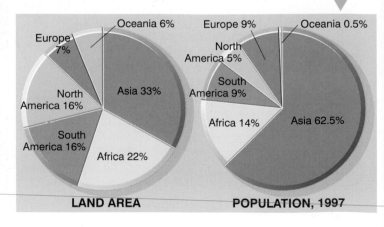

Oceania 6% Europe 9% Oceania 0.5%

Europe 7%

North America 5%

North America 16% Asia 33%

South America 9%

Africa 14%

South America 16% Asia 62.5%

Africa 22%

C

LAND AREA   **POPULATION, 1997**

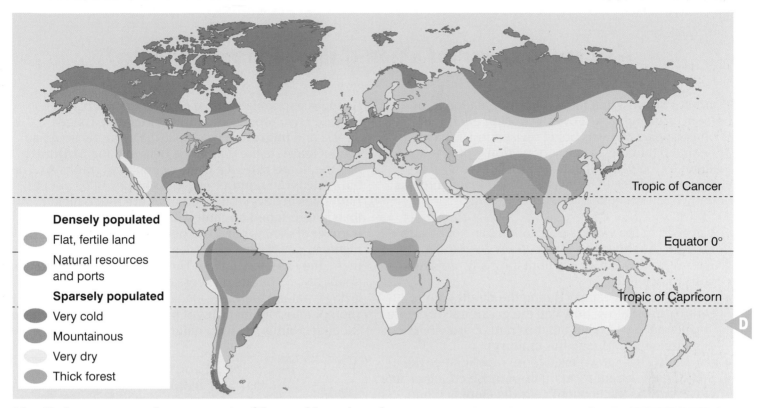

Densely populated
- Flat, fertile land
- Natural resources and ports

Sparsely populated
- Very cold
- Mountainous
- Very dry
- Thick forest

Tropic of Cancer

Equator 0°

Tropic of Capricorn

Map **D** gives reasons why some parts of the world are densely populated and other parts are sparsely populated. When looking at this map it should be realised that:

- it is very generalised and does not show local variations (e.g. it suggests, incorrectly, that *all* of a band across central Europe is densely populated and that *all* of rainforests in South America are sparsely populated).

- there are often several reasons, even if one is more important than the others, as to why a place is densely or sparsely populated (see *Connections* 66–68 and *Interactions* 84 map **A**).

Country	Area (km²)	Population (est.1997)	Density
Australia	7,713,360	18,400,000	
Brazil	8,511,970	159,500,000	
China	9,596,960	1,210,000,000	
Egypt	1,001,450	63,000,000	
Italy	301,270	57,750,000	
Japan	377,800	125,900,000	
Kenya	580,370	31,900,000	
Singapore	618	2,990,000	

Activities

1. **a)** Copy table **E** and complete the final column to show the population density of each country.
   b) Why are the population density figures misleading for: i) Brazil ii) Egypt?
   c) i) Why does China, which has more than one in five of the world's population, have a relatively low population density?
   ii) Why does Singapore, with a relatively small population, have such a high population density?
   iii) Why does England (376 people per km²) have a much higher population density than Scotland (70 people per km²)?

- Amazon Basin • Andes • Antarctica • Atacama
- Australia • Canadian Shield • China • Congo
- eastern USA • Ganges Basin and Bangladesh
- Gobi • Himalayas • Kalahari • Nile Valley
- northern Canada • north-west Europe • Rockies
- Sahara • south-east Brazil • Siberia

2. Map **F** gives the letters for six areas with a high population density (A to F) and numbers for 14 areas with a low, or sparse, population density (1 to 14). Using an atlas, or other geography textbooks, match the 20 areas in the following list with the appropriate letter or number.

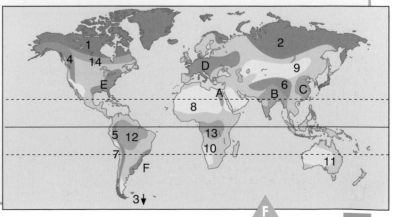

43

What are the causes and effects of changes in population size?

Estimates suggest that the world's population is, at present, growing by just over 90 million each year. When *Connections* was being revised in 1996, experts anticipated that the world's population would reach 6 billion by the year 2000 (page 70). Now, only three years later in 1999, these experts claim that figure has already been exceeded.

The growth in the world's population has not always been even. As shown on *Connections* 70 graph **A**, growth was slow but steady until the early nineteenth century. Since then:

- population grew rapidly during the nineteenth century in what we now call the economically more developed world (although this rate of growth has declined rapidly during this century)
- population has grown even more rapidly since the mid-twentieth century in many of those countries that we refer to as the economically developing world.

Changes in population size depend upon a balance between two processes: **natural increase** (pages 44–47) and **migration** (pages 50–53). Natural increase (or decrease) is the difference between the **birth rate** and the **death rate** of a place or country (graphs **A**). The birth rate is the number of live births per 1,000 people. Birth rates in developing countries are much higher than in developed countries. The death rate is the number of deaths per 1,000 people. Death rates are higher in developing countries although, in many of them, they are now falling. Throughout history there has nearly always been an excess of births over deaths giving a natural increase. Occasionally, and for only short periods during times of plague or war, deaths have exceeded births to give a natural decrease.

Developed countries

Growth rates	
1980–90	1990–95
0.9%	0.6%

Developing countries

Growth rates	
1980–90	1990–95
2.6%	1.9%

B

Wealth	1997 (est.)	Birth rate	Death rate	Natural increase	Infant mortality	Life expectancy
Increasing wealth	Japan	10	8	2	4	80
	Italy	10	10	0	7	79
	UK	13	11	2	6	77
	New Zealand	15	8	7	7	77
	Malaysia	26	5	21	23	70
	Brazil	20	9	11	53	62
	Egypt	28	9	19	71	62
	China	17	7	10	38	71
	India	25	9	16	69	60
Decreasing wealth	Kenya	32	11	21	55	55

Population also increases in economically developed countries where extra wealth enables more money to be spent on improving health care and diet. Improved health care and diet means that there is:

- a decrease in the **infant mortality rate** – the average number of deaths of children under one year of age per 1,000 live births
- an increase in **life expectancy** – the average number of years a person born in a particular country can expect to live.

Table **B** shows that more children survive and people can expect to live much longer in more wealthy, rather than in poorer, countries.

Population pyramids

The five factors shown in table **B** all affect the **population structure** of a country. Population structure can be shown by a **population pyramid** or, as it is sometimes known, an **age–sex pyramid** (graphs **C** and **D**). A population pyramid, which uses data ideally collected in a census, shows:

- the population of a country divided into five-year age-groups
- the percentage (proportion) of people in each age-group
- the percentage of males and females in each age-group.

Population pyramids are useful because they:

- allow comparisons to be made between countries, for example differences in their levels of economic development
- help to forecast future population trends (natural increase, birth rate, death rate, infant mortality rate, life expectancy) in order to predict future problems and planning needs, for example a growth in the elderly population may mean more residential homes are needed, or a growth in younger people may mean more schools will be required.

The shape of graph **C** is typical of many developed countries. The shape of graph **D** is more typical of developing countries.

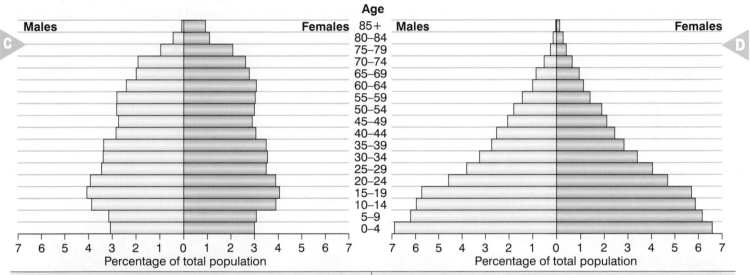

A low birth rate – relatively few children aged under 15	A high birth rate – a large number of children aged under 15
A low infant mortality rate	A high infant mortality rate
A straighter pyramid suggesting a lower death rate	A narrowing pyramid suggesting a higher death rate
Few people in the reproductive age-group (20–39) suggesting fewer children and a slow natural increase in population	Many people in the reproductive age-group (20–39) suggesting more children and a rapid increase in population
A longer life expectancy means more people reach old age	A shorter life expectancy means fewer people reach old age

Activities

1 a) What is meant by the terms:
 i) birth rate ii) death rate
 iii) natural increase iv) infant mortality
 v) life expectancy?

 b) Why do developed countries usually have: _(lower)_
 i) a higher birth rate
 ii) a lower infant mortality rate
 iii) a smaller natural increase
 iv) a longer life expectancy
 than developing countries?

2 Copy and complete table **E** by interpreting graphs **C** and **D**.

3 If you have access to the Internet, you can obtain the latest population figures for *any* country by using the following web site:

http://www.odci.gov/cia/publications/factbook

	Developed country C	Developing country D
% males aged under 4 years		
% total population aged under 15 years		
% total population aged over 65 years		
% females aged over 85 years		
Three age groups with highest % of population		
Shape of pyramid		

What are the effects of changes in population size?

Differences between developed and developing countries

Birth rates often depend upon economic (that is, wealth or poverty), religious and social factors. Figure **A** suggests why many developing countries have a much higher birth rate than do most developed countries. The UN and other world agencies have, for several decades, tried to encourage less well-off countries to reduce their birth rates (extract **B**).

However, while birth rates are indeed falling in almost every country, the rate of fall is often considered not to be fast enough (extract **C**).

Figure **A** also shows that death rates and life expectancy are similarly affected by economic and social factors. There is increasing concern in several developed countries, such as Sweden and Italy, where the birth rate is lower than the death rate and the total population is now declining. The consequence of a natural decrease in population is given in extract **D**.

We need many children:
- to help us work on the land and to carry wood and water,
- to care for us when we are ill or old and cannot work,
- because so many die from disease.
Four of my eight children died before their first birthday.

One child might get a job in the city and send us money. My religion forbids birth control. Having a big family increases my importance in the village.

Both my parents died when they were quite young. My mother died during a famine. My father caught cholera from dirty water. There was no hospital near and we could not afford medical care.

Both my parents are still alive. They live near to a doctor and a hospital. Their home has central heating. They are very comfortable.

Family planning controls the size of our family. We only wanted two children and we are sure they will live a long life, free from disease. We can afford to spend more money on our car, holidays and entertainment. We have pensions for when we are old. I wanted to return to my career and not stay at home.

A

Developing countries, e.g. India, Bangladesh, Kenya
Birth rates are high often because people want and need large families. The relatively short life expectancy is more likely to result from a lack of wealth.

Developed countries, e.g. UK, Sweden, Italy
Birth rates are low often because people do not need many children and prefer small families. The longer life expectancy results from the greater amount of wealth which is available.

B

Birth control in India
Unless India can reduce its birth rate, its population will exceed 2 billion and that of China's, by 2035. India's population control efforts so far have failed. The aim was to have two children per family by the year 2000, but the figures so far are double that.
Social workers have found the best contraceptive not to be condoms, the Pill, or sterilisation, but female literacy. Couples living in high-literacy states, especially those where girls have also had an education, tend to have only two children. In the more populous states where fewer people can read, families still have more than five children.

The United Nations state that there are two basic needs which must be accepted if birth rates are to be reduced:
- improving the status of women and allowing them to decide between having more children or birth control
- providing better education, especially for women, on family planning.

As death rates fall and life expectancy increases, then more people live longer. This in turn leads to an increase in demand for more money for pensions, medical care, residential homes and other social services. Where the death rate falls below the birth rate, the total population will begin to decrease. In time this will reduce the number of people available to work and to provide for the increasing number of elderly people.

Case Study

Population policies in China

1950s	High birth rate encouraged.
1956–60	Great famine.
1960s	High birth rate. Population grew by 55 million per year (total size of the UK).
1970s	Family planning programme introduced. Population grew by 40 million per year. Average family still over 3 children.
1979	One child per family policy. Families with one child got free education, priority housing, pensions and family benefits. Those with two children lost those concessions and were fined.
1980s	Population still grew by up to 25 million per year due to large numbers in reproductive age groups (20–39). Many single children spoilt – 'little emperors and empresses'. Some female infanticide. Many forced abortions. Rapid growth in ageing population. Shortage of females.
1990s	Some relaxation. Two children in rural areas if first was a girl. Two in other areas if first was disabled. Small ethnic groups were exempt. Annual population growth averaged 13.5 million.
1996	Further controls and inducements made.

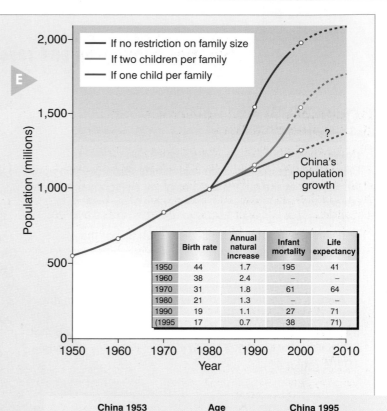

- If no restriction on family size
- If two children per family
- If one child per family

China's population growth

	Birth rate	Annual natural increase	Infant mortality	Life expectancy
1950	44	1.7	195	41
1960	38	2.4	–	–
1970	31	1.8	61	64
1980	21	1.3	–	–
1990	19	1.1	27	71
(1995	17	0.7	38	71)

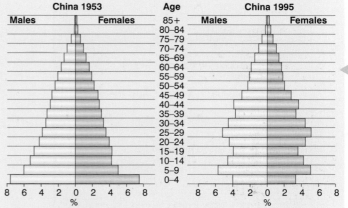

China 1953   Age   China 1995

Activities

1 With reference to pages 45–46, and to *Places* 43 and 91:
   a) Describe the differences in population growth, birth rate, death rate and infant mortality between Japan (a developed country) and Kenya (a developing country).
   b) Why has Japan, the more developed country, an ageing population?
   c) Why has Kenya, the less developed country, so many people aged under 15?

2 a) Why did China introduce its one child per family policy?
   b) What have been i) the advantages ii) the disadvantages of the policy?
   c) How has the one child policy affected China's population pyramid (graphs **E** and **F**)?
   d) Do *you* think Chinese parents should *either*: i) have the individual freedom to choose how many children they have *or* ii) restrict the size of their family for the good of the state?

Are population and resources interrelated?

Case Study

China

China is a huge country, with vast natural resources (diagram **A**). **Resources** are natural features of the environment that are needed and used by people, for example trees, fresh water, soil, fuels and minerals. However:

- neither the resources available (graph **B**) nor the distribution of people are evenly spread across the country (map **A** page 42 and map **C**)
- the rapid growth in China's population has meant that there is an increasing gap between population size and the resources available.

It was the concern, especially, about this widening gap that led to the introduction of China's one child policy in the late 1970s (page 47).

In the 1970s it was calculated that China's **optimum population** was 700 million. Using its simplest definition, optimum population is when there is a balance between the number of people and the resources available to them. Figure **E** on page 47 shows that China's population exceeded 700 million in about 1971. Since then, China is said to have been **overpopulated** – that is, the number of people living in the country exceeds the availability of resources (photo **D**). China expects its present population of 1,210 million (1997) to rise to a peak of 1,500 (2025) before falling. Even so, the eventual population is likely to remain at twice the optimum (2080).

A

CHINA
7.1% of Earth's land surface
– 10% Earth's fresh water
– 8% Earth's plants and trees
– 5% Earth's fossil fuels
– 4% Earth's minerals
... BUT ...
20.9% of the Earth's population

Potential land use

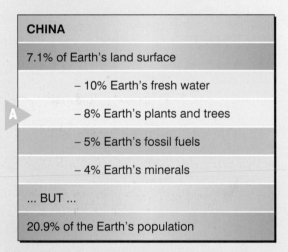

- 10% suitable as arable (crops)
- 14% forested
- 43% only suitable for pastureland
- 33% too dry or mountainous

B

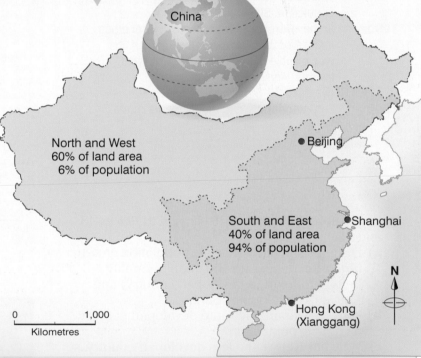

C

China

North and West
60% of land area
6% of population

Beijing

South and East
40% of land area
94% of population

Shanghai

Hong Kong
(Xianggang)

0   1,000
Kilometres

N

D

The world

In countries where there is a rapid population growth and/or consumption of resources, there is a danger of a fall in their standards of living. Countries that are underpopulated are those with insufficient people to make full use of the resources available. Overpopulation and underpopulation are very hard – if not impossible – to measure. This means that you may have formed an impression, or **perception**, of a country which may not be accurate because of:

- your lack of knowledge, e.g. do you know what resources places like Malaysia and China have?
- your assumption that all the country is the same, whereas often, as in the case of China and Brazil, some parts are overpopulated and other parts are underpopulated.

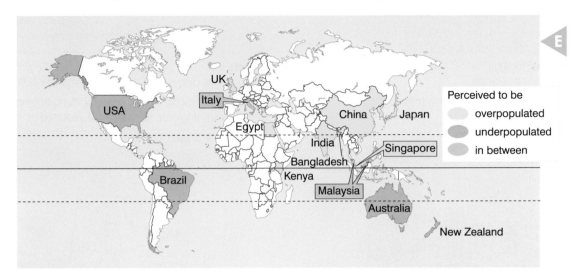

World rank	Country	Population size (thousands)	World rank	Country	Population density (per km²)	Country	Reasons why perceived to be either overpopulated or underpopulated
1	China	1,210,000	1	Singapore	5,426	Australia	Few people. Large country. Many resources.
2	India	980,000	4	Bangladesh	890	Bangladesh	Many people. Small country. Few resources.
3	USA	268,000	19	Japan	334	Brazil	Many people. Large country. Many resources.
5	Brazil	159,000	20	India	330	China	Many people. Large country. Average resources.
8	Japan	125,900	43	UK	243	Egypt	Many people in a small area. Few resources.
9	Bangladesh	124,000	50	Italy	196	India	Many people. Relatively few resources.
16	Egypt	63,000	68	China	129	Italy	Many people. Quite small country. Average resources.
21	UK	58,600	114	Malaysia	64	Japan	Many people. Small country. Few resources.
22	Italy	57,750	116	Egypt	63	Kenya	Many people. Few resources.
32	Kenya	31,900	126	Kenya	56	Malaysia	Many people. Few resources.
47	Malaysia	20,900	167	USA	28	New Zealand	Few people. Many resources.
51	Australia	18,400	181	Brazil	19	Singapore	Many people on small island. Few resources.
121	New Zealand	3,650	189	New Zealand	14	UK	Many people. Small country. Declining resources.
129	Singapore	3,200	226	Australia	2	USA	Many people. Large country. Vast resources.

Figures are for 1997

Activities

1 a) What is the difference between overpopulation and underpopulation?

   b) Explain why China is considered to be overpopulated.

2 a) Name two countries, other than China, that are **perceived** to be overpopulated. For each one, try to find out, with the help of other geographical resources, if indeed each country is overpopulated.

   b) Name two countries that are **perceived** to be underpopulated. For each one, try to find out, with the help of other geographical resources, if indeed each country is underpopulated.

What are the causes and effects of migration within a country?

Migration is the movement of people from one place to another, and usually means a change in home. Migration may be within a country (**internal migration**) or between countries (**external** or **international migration**); it may be for a short period of time or it can be permanent; and it may be **voluntary** (when people choose to move) or it can be **forced** (when people have no choice).

Causes ('push' factors)

Too few, or poorly-paid, jobs

Lack of services – few schools, hospitals, shops

Limited/non-existent public transport

and Effects

As people move out, some houses/farms are left deserted

With fewer inhabitants, small schools, hospitals and shops close and remaining bus services are reduced

Often an elderly population is left

RURAL–URBAN MIGRATION

and Effects

Local people are swamped by newcomers

House prices rise – become too expensive for local people to buy

New housing estates give villages a 'suburbanised' appearance

Insufficient places in local schools and hospitals

Traffic congestion/danger on narrow country lanes

Causes

Villages and smaller towns have a more healthy, cleaner and more attractive environment

New residential areas with larger houses and gardens

Modern industry prefers cleaner, out-of-town sites

Less pollution from traffic and older industries

Activities

1 **a)** A family who have moved from rural central Wales to live in London are said to be 'internal, permanent, voluntary migrants'. Explain carefully what this term means.

   b) Conduct a quick survey of your class to find out:
   i) how many have moved home
   ii) how often they have moved home
   iii) where they have previously lived.

   c) With the help of an atlas, locate on an outline map of Britain the places where members of your class have previously lived. (In some cases, depending on the answers to **b)** iii), the map might have to be of Europe or the world).

2 Divide your geography class into four groups. Each group should be given one of the following four questions.

Internal migration in the UK

In nineteenth-century Britain, many people moved from villages and small towns in rural areas to larger towns and cities, a process known as **rural–urban migration** (read from left to right along the top of the diagram below). Rural–urban migration, which still takes place in more isolated parts of Britain, is very common in many economically less developed countries (*Connections* 72–73). More recently in Britain, however, there has been a reversed process, known as **urban–rural migration**, where people have been leaving large cities and returning to smaller settlements (read from right to left along the bottom of the diagram below).

Causes ('pull' factors)
More and better-paid jobs

Better and more services – schools, hospitals and shops

Often a greater choice of housing

To be with members of own family or similar ethnic group already living there

'Bright lights' – entertainment, social and cultural amenities

and Effects
Overcrowding leading to increased demand/competition for houses, jobs, school places and hospital beds

Increase in traffic congestion and pollution

Increase in crime and vandalism

Potential problems associated with ethnic minorities

URBAN–RURAL MIGRATION

and Effects
Often it is the elderly, disabled, less skilled who are left

Old industrial sites left derelict

Old housing areas become run-down

Environmental problems and health risks due to pollution from traffic, rivers and the air

Causes
Overcrowding in schools, waiting lists for hospitals

Traffic congestion and other environmental and health problems

Industry and new shopping centres moving from inner city areas to edge-of-city/rural locations

a) i) Why do some people want to leave villages?
   ii) What effect does their movement have on the village?

b) i) Why do some people want to move to large cities?
   ii) What effect does their movement have on the large city?

c) i) Why do some people want to leave large cities?

   ii) What effect does their movement have on the large city?

d) i) Why do some people want to move to villages?
   ii) What effect does their movement have on the village?

Each group should then appoint a spokesperson to give their answers to the other groups.

What are the causes and effects of migration between countries?

The movement of people from one country to another is known as **international migration**. Those people who leave a country are referred to as **emigrants**, while those who arrive are called **immigrants**. The **migration balance** is the difference between the number of emigrants and the number of immigrants. Countries like the USA which gain more people by immigration than they lose through emigration will have an increase in their total population. Other countries, like the former Yugoslavia during the early 1990s, that lose more people through emigration than they gain by immigration, will have a decrease in their total population.

Voluntary migration is when people choose to move. This may be:	**Forced migration** is when people have little or no choice but to move. This may be the result of:
• to improve their standard of living, e.g. to find more or better-paid jobs	• natural disasters, e.g. earthquakes, volcanic eruptions or floods
• to improve their quality of life, e.g. retiring to a better climate, living and working either in a more pleasant environment or where there are better services.	• economic, social and political pressures, e.g. war, famine, religious or political persecution.

A

Causes

International migration can either be **voluntary** or **forced** (table **A**).

Map **B** shows some international movements into and out of Britain, and whether these movements were mainly voluntary or forced.

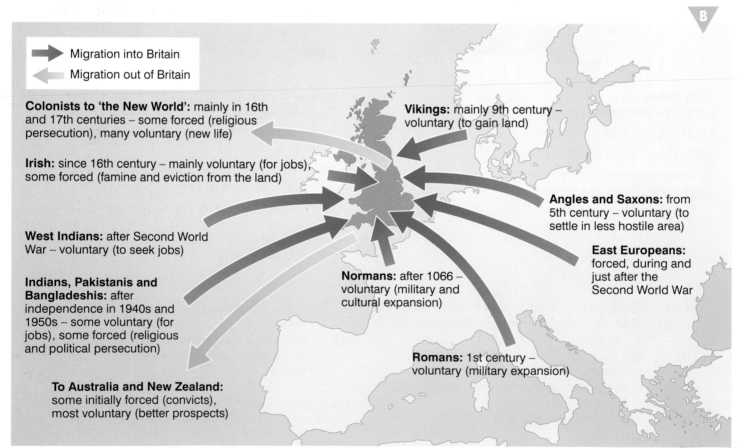

B

Migration into Britain
Migration out of Britain

Colonists to 'the New World': mainly in 16th and 17th centuries – some forced (religious persecution), many voluntary (new life)

Irish: since 16th century – mainly voluntary (for jobs), some forced (famine and eviction from the land)

West Indians: after Second World War – voluntary (to seek jobs)

Indians, Pakistanis and Bangladeshis: after independence in 1940s and 1950s – some voluntary (for jobs), some forced (religious and political persecution)

To Australia and New Zealand: some initially forced (convicts), most voluntary (better prospects)

Vikings: mainly 9th century – voluntary (to gain land)

Angles and Saxons: from 5th century – voluntary (to settle in less hostile area)

East Europeans: forced, during and just after the Second World War

Normans: after 1066 – voluntary (military and cultural expansion)

Romans: 1st century – voluntary (military expansion)

Effects

Migration on a large scale can affect the shape of population pyramids (see page 45). Graph **C** shows the effects on a country that gains more people through immigration than it loses by emigration. Graph **D** shows the effects on a country that loses more through emigration than it gains by immigration.

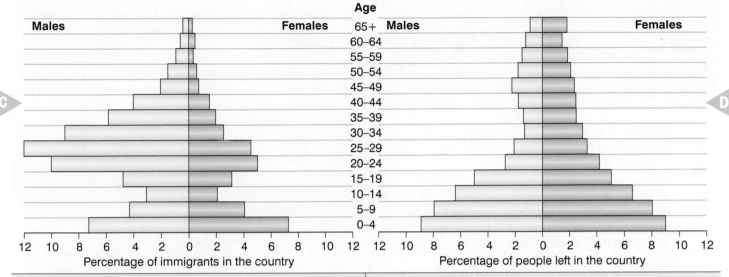

Percentage of immigrants in the country

Percentage of people left in the country

• Most migrants are aged between 20 and 39 years.	• Small numbers aged between 20 and 39 years because many have migrated.
• More males migrate than females (wives and children may migrate later to join their husbands).	• Fewer males than females left, as they tend to be the ones who migrate first to look for work.
• High birth rate as most migrants are in the reproductive age-group.	• High birth rate as country tends to be economically less developed.
• Relatively few elderly people migrate.	• High proportion in older age-groups as they tend not to migrate.

Activities

1 a) What is the difference between voluntary and forced migration?

b) Which of the following migrations are/were forced and which were/are voluntary?
- West Indians to the UK after the Second World War
- Mexicans into the USA
- The Normans into Britain in 1066 AD
- Sikhs into Britain
- Migrants from the former Yugoslavia in the 1990s
- Elderly, wealthy British spending winters in Spain
- Palestinian Arabs from Israel
- People from Montserrat after the volcanic eruption

2 With reference to graphs **C** and **D**:
a) Give four differences in the shape of the population pyramids.
b) Give four reasons for these differences.

3 Graph **E** shows the source of immigrants into Britain in the mid-1990s.
a) From where did most immigrants come? Give two reasons for your answer.
b) Excluding the 'Rest of Asia', from where did the second greatest number of immigrants come? Give a reason for your answer.
c) Name three areas from each of which Britain received 6 per cent of its total immigrants. For each place give a reason why people migrated to Britain.

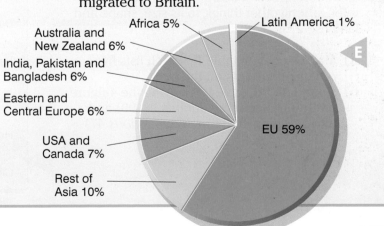

Africa 5%
Latin America 1%
Australia and New Zealand 6%
India, Pakistan and Bangladesh 6%
Eastern and Central Europe 6%
USA and Canada 7%
Rest of Asia 10%
EU 59%

What factors determine the site, functions and growth of a settlement?

Geographers can obtain important information about settlements by using maps and photographs. The following activities should extend your understanding of settlements (*Foundations* 44–47) and your ability to interpret maps (*Foundations* Unit 7) and photos (*Foundations* 10).

Activities

The following activities are based on the aerial photograph **A** and the Ordnance Survey map extract of Scarborough opposite.

1 **a)** In which direction was the camera pointing when the photograph was taken?
b) Three buildings have been labelled A, B and C on the photo. Find each one on the map and say what it is.
c) List three physical features and three human features (other than buildings A, B and C) which are shown on both the map and the photo.

2 *Foundations* 44–45 explains that settlements have different functions.
a) What do you think was the original function of Scarborough?
b) What other functions are suggested from the map and photo?

3 *Foundations* 46 explains how sites for settlements were chosen.
a) Where do you think the original site of Scarborough was located?
b) What natural advantages of the site of Scarborough are shown on the map and photo?

4 Using map and photo evidence *only*, write a short description of Scarborough. You might refer, among other things, to its size, shape and land use.

5 **a)** Make a copy of table **B**, which lists five other settlements on the map.
b) Complete the table by i) giving the 4-figure grid reference (*Foundations* 98–99) and ii) describing its shape (*Foundations* 47).

Settlement	4-figure grid reference	Shape
Burniston		
East Ayton		
Seamer		
Hutton Buscel		
Cloughton		

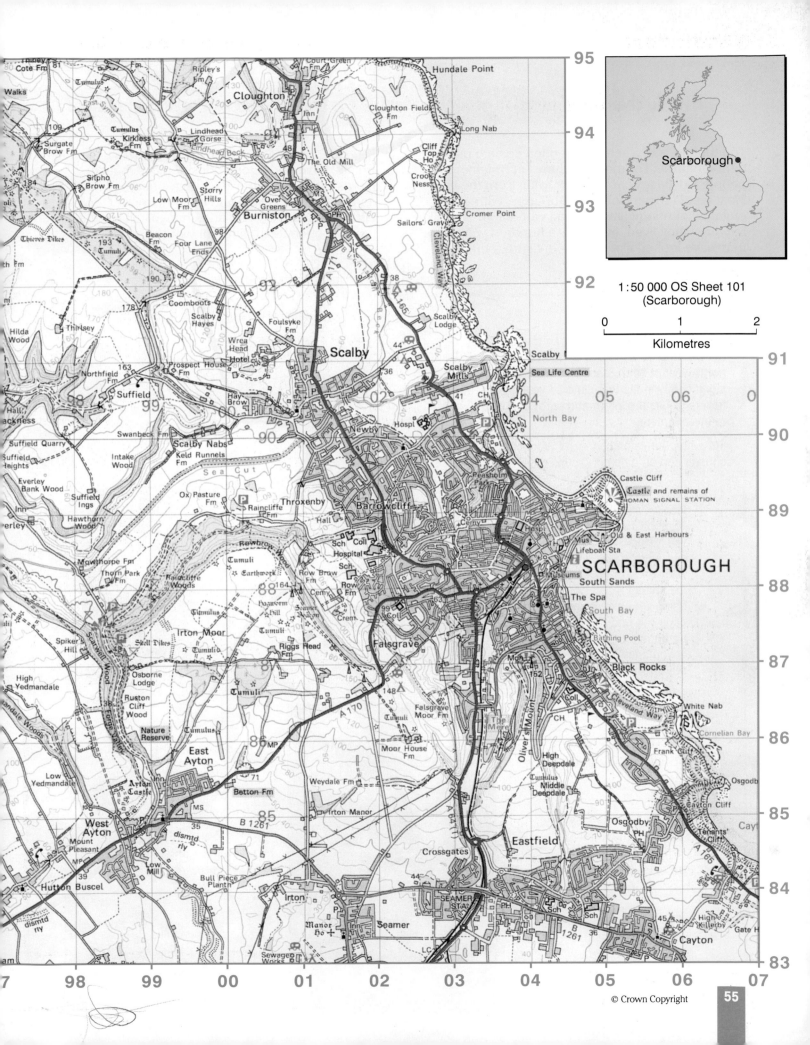

1:50 000 OS Sheet 101
(Scarborough)

0   1   2
Kilometres

Scarborough

SCARBOROUGH

© Crown Copyright

55

How do changes in function occur and how do they affect different groups of people?

The functions of a settlement often change over a period of time. For many centuries in Britain, most people in villages earned their living from the land. Most were farmers, or farm labourers, with a few engaged in mining and tending woodland. The village in which they lived, even only a hundred years ago, may have looked like the one in figure **A** on

Foundations 50. Since then it, and villages like it all over Britain, have undergone considerable change (*Foundations* 50 figure **B**). Villages near to large towns and cities have grown and become more **suburbanised**. Growth and change can affect different groups of people in different ways.

Enquiry

The village of Burniston (grid square 0093 on the OS map on page 55) is located 6.5 km north-west of Scarborough. It has changed significantly in the last hundred years. Your task is to use the information provided here to investigate:

'How has Burniston changed? What effect has change had on different groups of villagers?'

1 a) Using the map on page 55, draw a labelled sketch map of Burniston (see *Foundations* 106 diagram **B**). Make sure you include: the contour pattern of the surrounding hills, the shape of the village, Lindhead Beck, Burniston Beck, the roads.

b) Using your sketch map, the map on page 55, and *Foundations* 46, write a paragraph describing the 'natural advantages of the site of Burniston'.

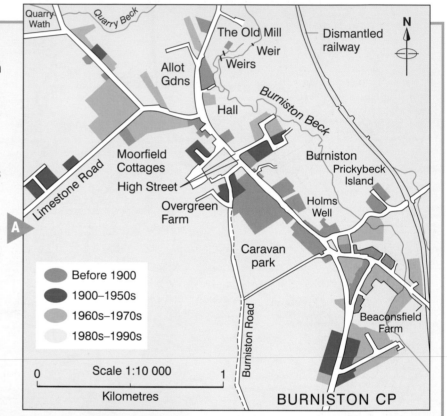

A

Key:
- Before 1900
- 1900–1950s
- 1960s–1970s
- 1980s–1990s

Scale 1:10 000

Kilometres

BURNISTON CP

B

Roofing material
Slate or clay tiles?

Building material
Brick, stone or pebble-dash?

Gutters and drainpipes
What are they made of? Do they look old?

Style design of building
Does it look old or new? Does it have a date on it?

Windows – style and type
Sash or bay?

Does the building have front/back gardens and/or a garage?

2 Map **A** shows the age of buildings in Burniston. It was drawn by plotting the findings of a school fieldwork investigation onto a 1:10 000 OS map. Many pupils found it difficult to estimate the age of buildings and so they were given figure **B** to help them with their task. How do the results of their fieldwork show how Burniston has changed?

3 The pupils also conducted research in Scarborough library and obtained the census data given in figures **C** and **D**.
  a) Draw a line graph to show population change in Burniston 1801–1994 (figure **C**). If you have access to a computer, you could produce a spreadsheet and chart.
  b) Describe how the population of Burniston has changed.
  c) i) Using the census data for Scarborough and Burniston in figure **D**, *either* draw two pie charts to show the differences between the settlements *or*, if you have access to a computer, produce spreadsheets and charts.
    ii) Describe, and try to give reasons for, any similarities and differences between the two settlements.

5 Write a short conclusion summarising the two enquiry questions:
  a) How has the village changed?
  b) How has change affected different groups of villagers?

C

Burniston population 1801–1994					
1801	246	**1871**	368	**1951**	613
1811	260	**1881**	353	**1961**	556
1821	347	**1891**	332	**1971**	871
1831	317	**1901**	308	**1981**	1,195
1841	329	**1911**	268	**1991**	1,430
1851	332	**1921**	298	**(1994**	1,390)
1861	350	**1931**	445		

D

1991 Census: car ownership, percentage of households		
	Scarborough	*Burniston*
Households with no car	48.7	18.7
Households with 1 car	41.2	50.1
Households with 2 or more cars	10.1	31.2
1991 Census: housing type, percentage of houses		
	Scarborough	*Burniston*
Detached	8.5	50.8
Semi-detached	20.7	37.9
Terraced	34.1	7.0
Purpose-built flat	15.7	4.3
Other	19.7	0
Shared dwelling	1.3	0

4 a) Read carefully the three newspaper extracts in figure **E**. According to the extracts:
    i) What are the advantages of living in Burniston?
    ii) How is the village changing?
  b) Change can be an advantage to some groups of people and can create problems for other groups. How is change in Burniston likely to affect the following people?
  ● a farmer
  ● a developer
  ● a local shopkeeper
  ● a conservationist
  ● an elderly resident
  ● a school-leaver
  ● a young couple about to get married

E

Old and new together

TYSON Halder has farmed in Burniston since 1939. Leslie Birch moved to the village two years ago.

Mr Halder still identifies with the core of the village as a community – but things are changing with the spread of new housing.

'At one time, you used to know everybody – all the schoolchildren, the lot. Now we know the neighbours around and that's about it – a lot of new buildings have gone up, and a lot of new people have come in. It's not quite the village it used to be.

'Some of the new people want it to be like a town – they complain about farming smells, about the lane being dirty when the cows go down. At one time there were only the cows, now there are people too.'

'You don't have to look for character in this village, it's all around you,' said Mr Birch.

'The homeliness is there, the kindness of life is there, and everything about giving to each other is there.

'I wouldn't live in a place like Scarborough with all the crowds and the traffic – it would kill me.

'This is a lovely place, it's a real home to me; and it's the villagers who have made me feel that way.'

Village outcry over housing

Burniston parish councillors have voiced their 'total opposition' to the plans of a local developer to build 14 new homes in the area.

Around 20 members of the public arrived at a meeting of the Parish Council when fears were expressed about the planning application submitted by Beckenby Estates Ltd.

Concern was voiced that the land for the 14 new homes plan was used as farmland for grazing cattle and that the proposed accesses would not be satisfactory.

The parish council agreed that they should point out that the land is within the rural landscape protection area and is not allocated as residential use in the Scarborough Local Plan.

Members were also concerned that the sewage system in the village would not be able to cope with the extra housing, and that the extra traffic would be a difficulty.

Fears of housing explosion in Burniston

RESIDENTS in Burniston fear the village is being developed too quickly, a councillor has warned.

People of the village are worried that housing developments are taking place too quickly, Councillor Michael Pitts told a meeting of Scarborough Council's Development sub-committee for the central-rural area.

Source: *Scarborough Evening News*

How do types and variety of goods and services differ between settlements of different sizes?

If you have read *Foundations* 56, you should be familiar with the term **settlement hierarchy**. This is when settlements are put into an order based upon either their population size, their distance apart, or the types and variety (range) of goods and services they provide.

You should, however, be aware of two new terms: the **threshold population** and the **range of goods and services**.

- The **threshold population** is the minimum number of people needed for a service to be provided. Fewer people are needed for a village shop, public house or primary school to remain open than for a supermarket, bank or secondary school.

- The **range of goods or a service** is the maximum distance that people are prepared to travel for those goods or service. People will travel much further to buy furniture and clothes (goods) or to see a doctor (a service) than to buy a daily newspaper.

Map **A** is based on a 1 : 50 000 OS map (Sheet 86 Haltwhistle) and shows twelve settlements located to the east of Carlisle. The map shows, based on fieldwork, the types and number of services available in each settlement.

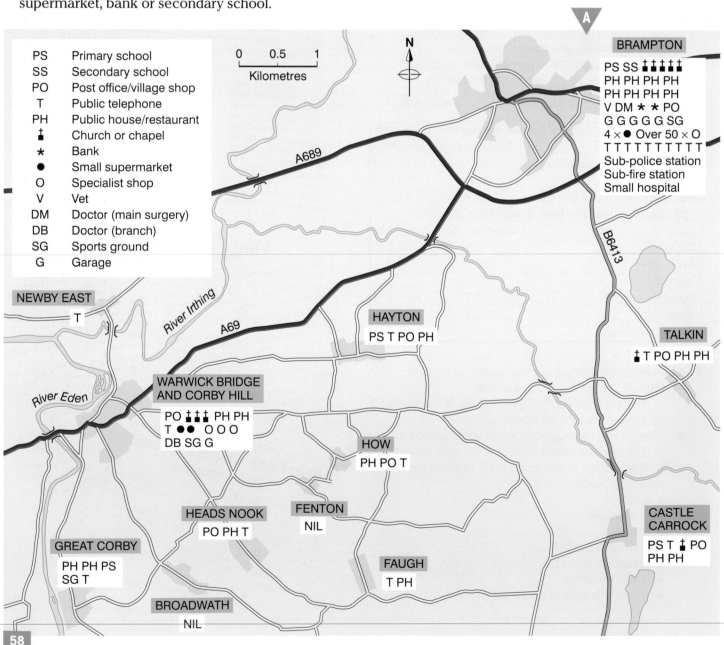

PS	Primary school
SS	Secondary school
PO	Post office/village shop
T	Public telephone
PH	Public house/restaurant
♱	Church or chapel
★	Bank
●	Small supermarket
O	Specialist shop
V	Vet
DM	Doctor (main surgery)
DB	Doctor (branch)
SG	Sports ground
G	Garage

BRAMPTON
PS SS ♱♱♱♱♱
PH PH PH PH
PH PH PH PH
V DM ★ ★ PO
G G G G G SG
4 × ● Over 50 × O
T T T T T T T T T
Sub-police station
Sub-fire station
Small hospital

NEWBY EAST
T

HAYTON
PS T PO PH

TALKIN
♱ T PO PH PH

WARWICK BRIDGE AND CORBY HILL
PO ♱♱♱ PH PH
T ● ● O O O
DB SG G

HOW
PH PO T

HEADS NOOK
PO PH T

FENTON
NIL

CASTLE CARROCK
PS T ♱ PO
PH PH

GREAT CORBY
PH PH PS
SG T

FAUGH
T PH

BROADWATH
NIL

Activities

1 a) Make copies of table **B** and diagram **C**.
  b) Complete your copy of table **B** by using information given on map **A**.
  c) i) Complete your copy of diagram **C** by giving examples obtained from table **B**.
  ii) Perhaps you found one or two settlements difficult to fit into one of the four categories. Why was this?

d) With regard to goods and services, what are the advantages and/or disadvantages of living in:
  • Fenton
  • Castle Carrock
  • Warwick Bridge
  • Brampton?

Settlement	Total no. of services available	No. of different services available	No. of services listed in key to map **A** which are not available	Type of settlement (hamlet, small village, large village, small town)
Brampton				
Broadwath				
Castle Carrock	6	5	8	small village
Faugh				
Fenton				
Great Corby				
Hayton				
Heads Nook				
How				
Newby East				
Talkin				
Warwick Bridge				

2 Diagram **D** shows distances travelled by people to three settlements in order to obtain goods and services. Match the three places, X, Y and Z with the goods and services given in the following list.
  • doctor
  • daily newspaper at the village shop
  • primary school
  • secondary school
  • public house
  • petrol at a garage
  • small supermarket
  • specialist shop, e.g. chemist or florist

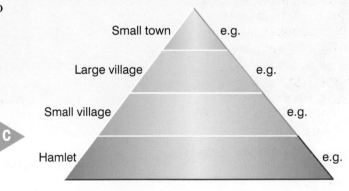

Small town   e.g.

Large village   e.g.

Small village   e.g.

Hamlet   e.g.

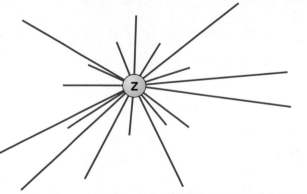

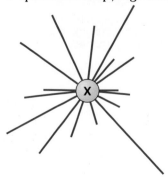

What are the main types and patterns of urban land use?

It has been stated earlier in this book that geographers are interested in **patterns**. One of the best-known geographical patterns is that showing land use in a typical British city. This land use pattern, known as the Burgess model, is explained in *Foundations* 52–53. Figures **A–D** below allow you to study the model in more detail, as they show sections of OS maps together with matching aerial photographs and diagrams.

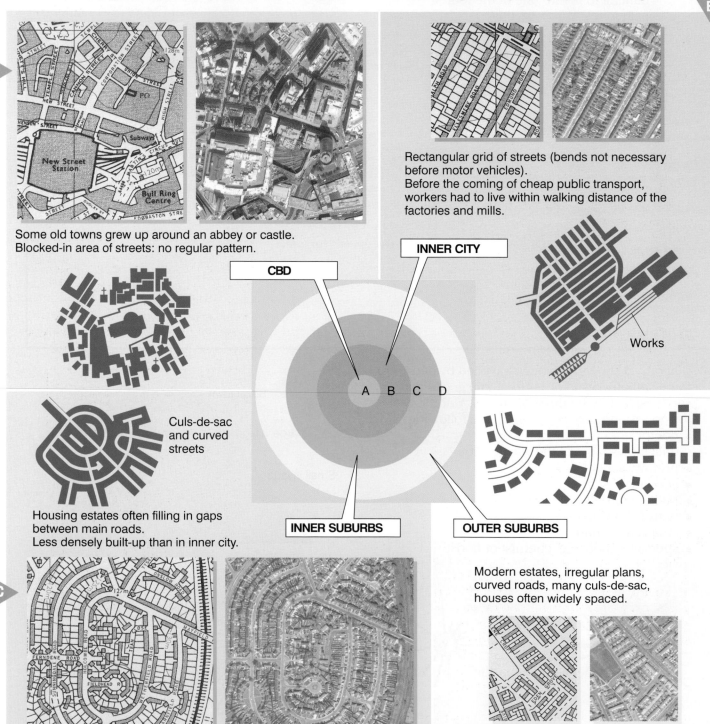

A

Some old towns grew up around an abbey or castle.
Blocked-in area of streets: no regular pattern.

B

Rectangular grid of streets (bends not necessary before motor vehicles).
Before the coming of cheap public transport, workers had to live within walking distance of the factories and mills.

INNER CITY

Works

CBD

A B C D

C

Culs-de-sac and curved streets

Housing estates often filling in gaps between main roads.
Less densely built-up than in inner city.

INNER SUBURBS

OUTER SUBURBS

Modern estates, irregular plans, curved roads, many culs-de-sac, houses often widely spaced.

D

1 : 10,000 map extracts © Crown copyright

It is accepted that towns and cities do not grow in a haphazard way but rather they develop recognisable shapes and patterns. Although you should be aware that each town is unique, with its own pattern, it is likely to share characteristics with other towns. As in any geographical model, the Burgess land use model has simplified real-world situations and has made them easier to describe and to understand. It also gives a starting point to help you look at real cities.

Activities

1 a) Make a large copy of the circular diagram at the centre of figures **A–D** (or use *Foundations* 52 diagram **B**).
  b) Inside each zone, draw a simplified map to show the street layout (pattern).
  c) Under each of your maps, write one sentence to describe the main points of the layout (pattern).

2 The four extracts in figures **A–D** are all from 1 : 10 000 OS maps. The outlines of buildings and their gardens/yards can be seen quite clearly.
  a) For each of the four zones, draw or trace a sketch map to show the buildings and their gardens/yards.
  b) Calculate the building density of each zone. To do this you need to count the number of buildings on each sketch map (if more than half a building is on the map then count as one, if less than half then ignore – diagram **E**). Give your answer in buildings per hectare.
  c) Draw a graph, which could be computer-generated, to show your results.
  d) Describe what your results show.

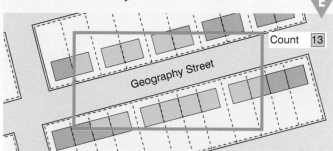

Count 13

Geography Street

E

3 You should now be able to identify land use patterns: i) by using OS maps at different scales (e.g. the 1 : 50 000 map) and ii) in your own local town and city. Although the following questions refer to the Scarborough map on page 55, you could ask similar questions using your local map.
  a) In which grid square, or squares, is Scarborough's Central Business District (CBD)?
  b) Give the 6-figure grid reference (*Foundations* 100) for the: i) town hall ii) castle iii) railway station.
  c) Describe the type of housing likely to be found in grid squares: i) 0189 ii) 0388 iii) 0389.

4 a) As a class, obtain the 'Houses for Sale' section from your local newspaper and, if some of you have a camera, take photographs of houses in different parts of your local town or city.
  b) Cut out the property details from the newspaper and stick these, together with the photographs, in their correct location onto a (very) large map (possibly an OS map) of the town.
  c) Try to identify possible land use zones and draw a sketch map to show these zones. Remember to give the completed map a title and a key.
  d) Produce a poster showing the land use zones of your local settlement.
   i) Include the photographs and property details that you have collected, together with copies of large-scale maps of different zones, and a map of the whole settlement.
   ii) Label the photographs and maps to identify key features of each area, as suggested in *Foundations* 53 diagram **C**.
  If possible, refer to the land use model. Try to demonstrate on your poster whether your local settlement matches the Burgess land model.

5 Use a CD-ROM to research aerial photographs and/or maps of different land uses in towns or cities (e.g. Discover London, Discover York). You could paste the resources into a desktop publishing program to show the characteristic features of the land use area.

What conflicts can arise over urban land use?

Map **A** is based on the 1:50 000 OS map of Scarborough (see page 55). Like *Foundations* 60 diagram **A**, it shows main roads and the railway leading into the centre of the town. This means that the town centre, or **Central Business District**, is the most **accessible** part of the urban area. People can get to it equally easily and quickly from any part of the town or the nearby settlements.

Because of its accessibility, many economic activities such as shops, offices and banks, consider the CBD to be the best place to locate. By locating here, each believes that they can attract the maximum number of customers. However, as the different types of activity compete with one another for space, then land prices are pushed up. The result is that **land values** in the CBD are always very high (quite often the site with the highest land value is occupied by a Marks & Spencer), and decrease rapidly with increasing distance from the town centre (diagram **B**). As the number of shops and offices locating within the CBD continued to increase, this led to greater numbers of shoppers and workers travelling to and from the CBD each day. This meant:

- increased traffic congestion along main roads leading into, and within, the CBD
- increased competition for land for road-widening schemes and for city-centre car parks
- increased competition between vehicles (cars, lorries and buses) and pedestrians within the CBD.

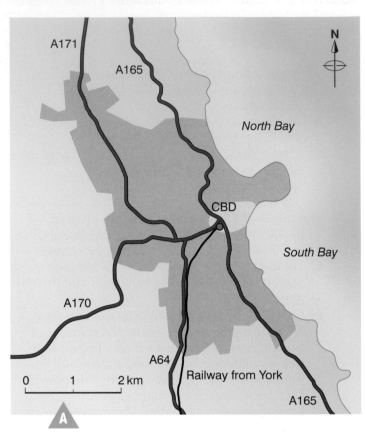

A

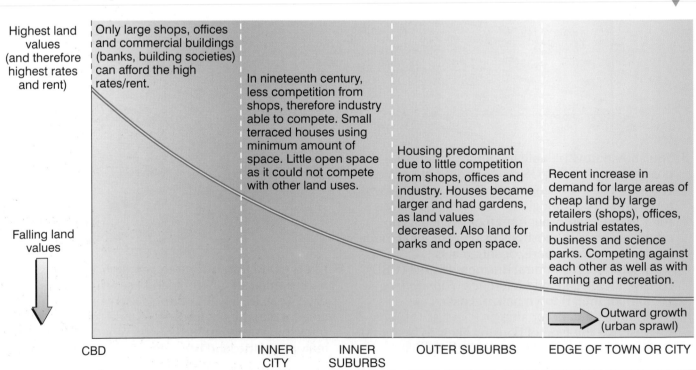

B

Highest land values (and therefore highest rates and rent)

Only large shops, offices and commercial buildings (banks, building societies) can afford the high rates/rent.

In nineteenth century, less competition from shops, therefore industry able to compete. Small terraced houses using minimum amount of space. Little open space as it could not compete with other land uses.

Housing predominant due to little competition from shops, offices and industry. Houses became larger and had gardens, as land values decreased. Also land for parks and open space.

Recent increase in demand for large areas of cheap land by large retailers (shops), offices, industrial estates, business and science parks. Competing against each other as well as with farming and recreation.

Falling land values

Outward growth (urban sprawl)

CBD   INNER CITY   INNER SUBURBS   OUTER SUBURBS   EDGE OF TOWN OR CITY

The two main types of land use near to the edge of a city have been housing and open space (e.g. parks). More recently, however, there has been increasing competition by large-scale shopping developments (e.g. MetroCentre, Meadowhall and Lakeside), office relocation, urban by-passes and the creation of industrial estates and business and science parks (photo **C**). These developments have taken advantage of cheaper land values, limited traffic congestion and a more pleasant environment (diagram **B**). This increase in competition at the so-called **urban–rural fringe** has led to the outward growth of cities, a process known as **urban sprawl**. Urban sprawl in turn competes with farmland and rural recreational amenities.

Activities

1 **a)** Find the OS map that shows your local town or city.
   b) Draw a sketch map for your local town or city similar to map **A**. Mark on and label:
   - the edge of the urban area
   - any railway in use
   - the main roads – make sure you add their number (e.g. A64) and the urban area to which they lead (e.g. to York).
   c) Based on your sketch map and your own personal knowledge, explain the problems caused in the CBD by the road and rail pattern.

2 **a)** Explain why: i) land values are high in the CBD
   ii) land values decrease rapidly towards the edge of the built-up area.
   b) Based on land values, put the following types of land use in order. Put the one (or ones) which you consider use the most expensive sites first.
   - banks and building societies
   - factories   • housing
   - hypermarkets and regional shopping centres
   - Premier League football ground
   - public parks   • science parks
   - shoe and clothes shops

3 Photograph **C** shows several types of land use at the edge of a British city. On a copy of sketch **D**, which is drawn from the photo, put labels for the following types of land use at the appropriate locations.
   - farmland   • housing   • wasteland
   - industrial estate   • motorway   • woodland

4 The newspaper headlines in figure **E** relate to conflicts over land use in cities. For one of the headlines or, preferably, a conflict that is occurring or has occurred in your local town or city:
   a) Describe the scheme.
   b) Give the views of people in favour of the scheme.
   c) Give the views of people against the scheme.
   d) What was (or is likely to be) the outcome?

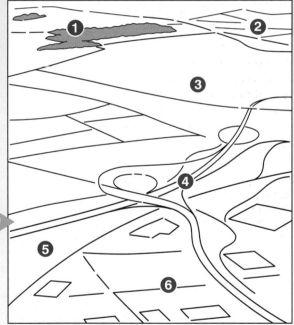

Hypermarket to be built on edge of playing fields

City park will lose land in road-widening scheme

Shopping complex and office development compete for prime site in city centre

Flats to be pulled down for new office block

Playing fields sold for large housing development

What are some solutions to conflicts over urban land use?

Case Study

Tokyo

Japan's population is not distributed evenly across the country. This is mainly because much of the country is mountainous and sparsely populated, and only a relatively small area is sufficiently flat and low-lying for farming, industry and settlement (map **A**). Most of Japan's 127 million inhabitants are crowded together on only 17 per cent of the total land area. Added to this, Japan's rapid growth in population size and in wealth since 1945 has led to tremendous competition for land use in large cities such as Tokyo and Osaka.

In 1996, the population of Greater Tokyo was estimated to be 28.6 million. Central Tokyo is crowded in terms of buildings and people (photo **B**). Some parts have the highest population density in the world, with over 20,000 people living in a square kilometre (page 42). Such overcrowding has, naturally, created problems for the authorities and for people living in Tokyo. Attempts to solve these problems include the following.

● **Trying to separate land-users in the city centre.** Tokyo, unlike most large cities, has several CBDs (map **C**), with each tending to specialise in one particular function, e.g. government offices (Shinjuku – *Places* 94 photo **B**), business and commerce (Marunouchi) and luxury shopping (Ginza – *Places* 94 photo **C**).

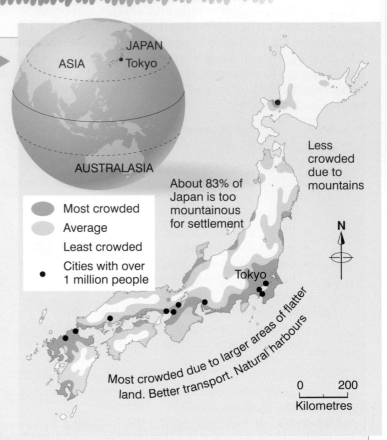

Less crowded due to mountains

About 83% of Japan is too mountainous for settlement

Most crowded

Average

Least crowded

● Cities with over 1 million people

Tokyo

Most crowded due to larger areas of flatter land. Better transport. Natural harbours

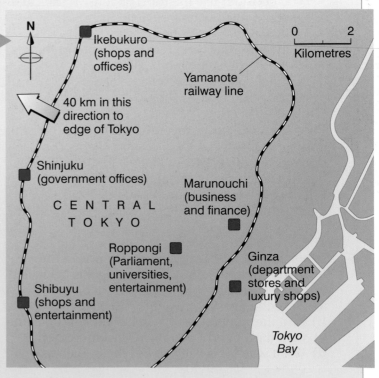

Ikebukuro (shops and offices)

Yamanote railway line

40 km in this direction to edge of Tokyo

Shinjuku (government offices)

CENTRAL TOKYO

Marunouchi (business and finance)

Roppongi (Parliament, universities, entertainment)

Ginza (department stores and luxury shops)

Shibuyu (shops and entertainment)

Tokyo Bay

D

E

- **Erecting high-rise buildings to offset high land values** Most government offices, constructed to be earthquake-proof, are situated in spectacular high-rise buildings in Shinjuku (photo **D**) while many Tokyo residents have to live in high-rise flats (photo **E**).

- **Trying to segregate pedestrians and traffic**, albeit only at weekends, in parts of the major shopping area of Ginza (photo **F**).

- **Creating a dense network of urban railways**, both on the surface and underground, to try to reduce the effects of road transport (extract **G**).

- **Reclaiming land from Tokyo Bay**, for industry, commerce, port facilities and high-rise apartments. One such development is described in *Places* 97 figure **D**).

- **Preventing building** within the grounds of the Imperial Palace, as this provides the only large area of open space in central Tokyo (*Places* 96 photo **B**).

F

G

'Each working day sees 15 million passenger journeys made by rail, 7 million by subways, 6 million by private car and 4 million by buses and taxis. The railway station at Shinjuku alone handles over 4 million passengers a day. It is so crowded that "pushers" are used to cram more people into trains. To save space, many roads run directly over, or under, railway lines. Many of the elaborate and expensive urban expressways have four lanes or more in each direction.'

Activities

1 a) Describe four ways in which the authorities in Tokyo have tried to solve some of the problems created by competition for land use in their city.

   b) Briefly comment upon how successful you think they have been.

2 The authorities in your local town or city are also likely to have tried to solve problems created by competition for land use. Briefly describe their schemes and say whether you think their efforts have been successful or not.

What is the difference between primary, secondary and tertiary activities?

  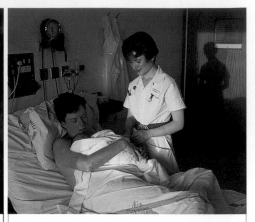

Primary activities involve **extracting** or collecting natural resources from the environment. These activities include farming, fishing, forestry, mining and quarrying.

Secondary activities take the raw materials obtained by primary activities and turn, or **manufacture**, them into various products which people can use. They include steelmaking, car assembly and the production of micro-chips.

Tertiary activities provide a **service** for people. They include activities that sell products made by secondary activities or which help people. Selling cars, teaching, nursing and tourist guiding are examples of this type of activity.

A

You will have already discovered on *Connections* 20 and 34 that people earn their living from different economic activities. It is usual to group these economic activities into three sectors (figure **A**).

Interactions 86 explains that the proportion of the population working in each economic sector is called the **employment structure**. Employment structures:
1 can change over a period of time (table **B**)
2 vary from place to place, i.e. between countries, or between regions and towns within countries.

For example, *Places* 10 identifies employment structure as an indicator of a country's development which may:
- change as a country develops economically (point 1 above)
- be used to differentiate between countries that are at different stages of economic development (point 2 above).

Activities

1 As a geographer you should still be building up your geographical vocabulary. Give the meaning of the terms:
   a) primary activities
   b) secondary activities
   c) tertiary activities
   d) employment structure.

2 a) Look through your local newspaper to find the 'Jobs vacant' section. Cut out the job vacancies and group them into the three sectors of the economy.

   b) Conduct a survey in your class to find out the types of job done by each pupil's family (parents, grandparents, brothers, sisters). Sort the information into the three sectors of the economy.
   c) Record, on a bar graph, the results obtained in activities **2a)** and **2b)**. You could use a computer and spreadsheet to chart your data.
   d) Describe your findings in activity **2c)**.
   e) Which employment sector is likely to attract you the most when you begin to look for a job? Give reasons for your answer.

3 Try to find out the main economic activities in your local area. Your teacher may have some statistics to help you, or you may need to visit the school library or local library to find census data for your area. Again, you could use a computer to chart any data that you may find.

4 Table **B** shows changes in the UK's employment structure between 1795 and 1995.
   a) Draw pie charts for each year. Use the same colours for the three sectors as used in figure **A** and remember to use the same colours on each chart. You could, again, use a computer spreadsheet and chart.
   b) Describe what your pie charts show.
   c) Try to think of some reasons for the changes over a period of time in the UK's employment structure.

5 Look carefully at figure **D**. It shows three imaginary economic regions within a country, and how economic activity varies from place to place. Figure **C** shows, in the form of pie charts, the employment structure for the three regions.
   a) Match each pie chart with its correct economic region.
   b) In each case give four pieces of evidence to support your choice.

B

Year	Primary	Secondary	Tertiary
1795	75%	15%	10%
1895	15%	55%	30%
1995	2%	28%	70%

6 a) To answer this part of the question you will have to refer to the 1 : 50 000 OS map of Scarborough on page 55.
Name the economic activity at each of the following grid references and say whether it is primary, secondary or tertiary.
   i) 984881   ii) 016887   iii) 996885
   iv) 008831   v) 030906   vi) 038888
   vii) 044884   viii) 036907

   b) Using the 1 : 50 000 OS map of Cambridge on *Foundations* 109, name:
   i) the three primary activities at each of 423541, 415590 and 443569
   ii) the two secondary activities at each of 482572 and 471497
   iii) the three tertiary activities at each of 452589, 467551 and 452516.

C

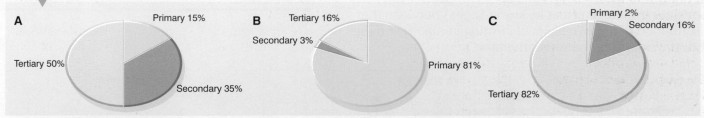

A — Primary 15%, Tertiary 50%, Secondary 35%

B — Tertiary 16%, Secondary 3%, Primary 81%

C — Primary 2%, Secondary 16%, Tertiary 82%

D

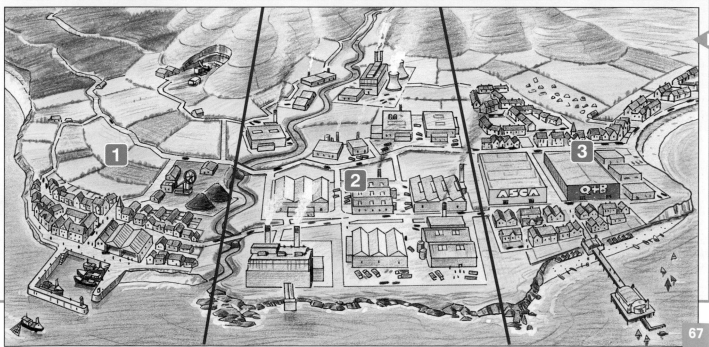

What is the geographical distribution of one type of primary activity?

The location and distribution of economic activities

All types of economic activity, whether primary, secondary or tertiary (service), depend upon a combination of **physical** (natural) and **human/ economic** (artificial) factors (table **A**). As we shall see in the next few pages, physical factors tend to be the more important in the location and distribution of primary activities, while human and economic factors tend to have a greater influence on the location of secondary and tertiary activities.

The distribution of a primary activity – sheep and cereal farming in the UK

As has already been stated earlier in this book, geographers are interested in **patterns** and **distributions**. Map **B** shows the generalised distribution of two types of farming – sheep and cereals (wheat and barley). Activity **1a)** asks you to look at the distribution of these two types of farming, and to try to identify any possible patterns. The four maps in figure **C** relate to four physical factors – rainfall, temperature, relief and land quality (soils). Activity **1b)** asks you to identify distribution patterns regarding each of these four factors. Geographers are also interested in **relationships**. Activity **1c)** asks if you can see any obvious relationship (that is, any linkages) between the distribution of the two types of farming in map **B** and the four physical factors shown in maps **C**.

Physical factors	
Climate	Rainfall
	Temperature
Relief	Height of land
	Shape/steepness of land
Soils	
Resources	Minerals
	Energy

Human/economic factors		
Markets	–	where goods are sold
Labour		Quantity and quality
		Wages
Capital	–	money available
Transport	–	types and cost
Technology	–	recent innovations
Government help	–	national, EU
Environment	–	attractiveness, nearness

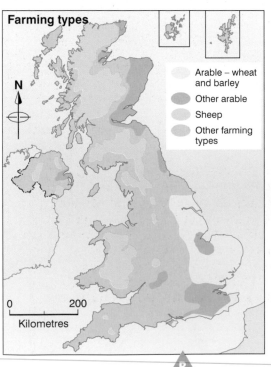

Farming types

Legend:
- Arable – wheat and barley
- Other arable
- Sheep
- Other farming types

0   200
Kilometres

B

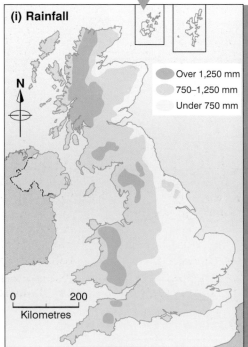

(i) Rainfall

Legend:
- Over 1,250 mm
- 750–1,250 mm
- Under 750 mm

0   200
Kilometres

C

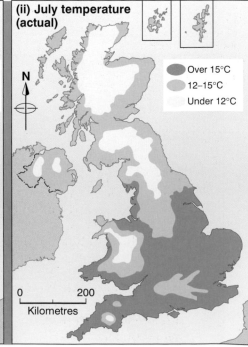

(ii) July temperature (actual)

Legend:
- Over 15°C
- 12–15°C
- Under 12°C

0   200
Kilometres

Changes in distribution

The basic pattern of sheep and cereal farming across the UK has changed little over the centuries. This is mainly because sheep farmers are more likely to live in an area (photo **D**) where the physical factors encourage the rearing of sheep and discourage the growing of cereals (*Connections* 24–25 and 29). Likewise, cereal farmers are likely to live in places (photo **E**) where physical factors are more suited to the growing of wheat and barley rather than the rearing of sheep (*Connections* 24–25 and 28).

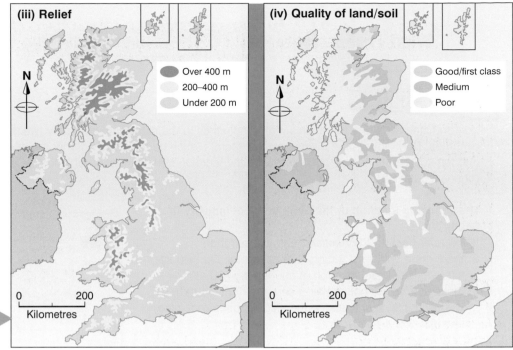

(iii) Relief

- Over 400 m
- 200–400 m
- Under 200 m

N

(iv) Quality of land/soil

- Good/first class
- Medium
- Poor

N

0 — 200 Kilometres

0 — 200 Kilometres

C

D

E

Activities

1 a) Describe any obvious patterns in the location and distribution of:
i) sheep   ii) cereals in the UK (map **B**).

b) Describe any obvious patterns in the location and distribution of:
  i) rainfall   ii) temperatures   iii) relief
  iv) land quality (soils) in the UK (figure **C**).

c) Write one sentence to describe any possible relationship between i) sheep and ii) cereals for each of the following:
• rainfall   • temperature   • relief
• land quality (soils).

2 a) What is the difference between i) physical and ii) human/economic factors?

b) With reference to the location and distribution of i) sheep farming and ii) cereal farming, explain why physical factors are usually more important than human/economic factors.

c) For *either* sheep farming *or* cereal farming, explain why its location and distribution have not changed significantly over the centuries.

What is the geographical distribution of one type of secondary activity?

Case Study

Iron and steel was one of Britain's major industries in the nineteenth and early twentieth centuries. During that time it was physical factors, such as the source of raw materials and the source of energy, that determined the location and distribution of industry (figure **A** page 68).

The changing location of the iron and steel industry in South Wales

If you refer back to *Connections*, you will see that:

- there are a variety of factors that determine the best site, or sites, for the initial location of an industry (36–37)
- these factors may alter over a period of time so that, as with Britain's steel industry, the ideal location may also change (38, 44–45).

In the late nineteenth century there were almost 150 small blast furnaces, using local coal and iron ore, making iron and steel in the Ebbw Vale area. By the 1960s, these had been replaced by two huge iron and steel works at Port Talbot and Llanwern (map **A**). The OS maps and aerial photos of Ebbw Vale (**B** and **C**) and Llanwern (**D** and **E**) provide evidence which should allow you to suggest reasons for the changing location of iron and steel in South Wales.

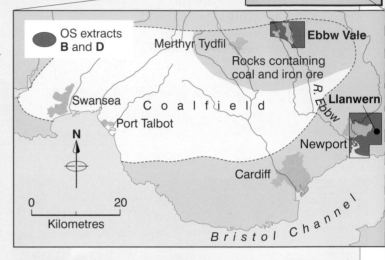

1 : 50 000 OS Sheet 171 Cardiff & Newport, showing Llanwern   © Crown Copyright

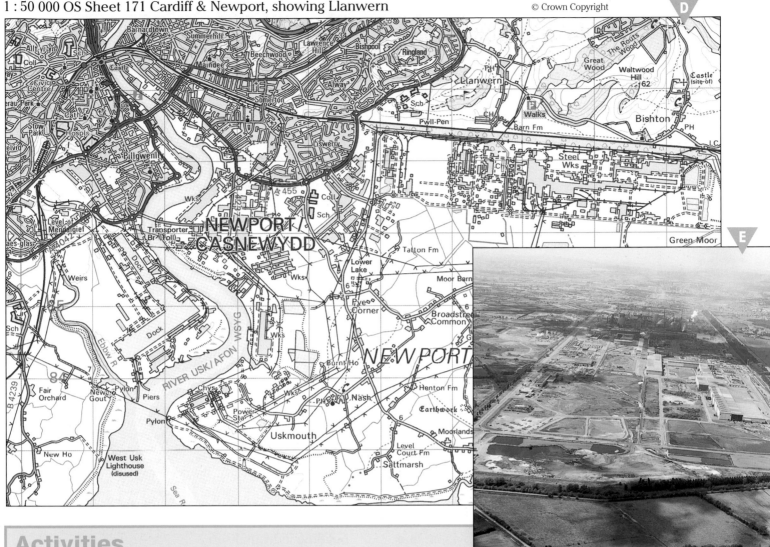

Activities

1 Look closely at maps **B** and **D** and photos **C** and **E**. Compare the two locations with sites W, X, Y and Z on diagram **A**, *Connections* 44. Which of the four sites do you think a) Ebbw Vale b) Llanwern resembles?

2 If you have already completed the Activities on *Connections* 44–45 you will have a good idea about how location factors for an industry, such as iron and steel, change through time. Remembering that there were ironworks in Ebbw Vale in the nineteenth century:
a) Using box **B** and matrix **C** in *Connections* 45, together with map **B** and photo **C** opposite, give Ebbw Vale a score for its site.
b) Give four reasons, with examples from the map and photo, why Ebbw Vale was a good site for a nineteenth-century ironworks.

3 By the 1950s Ebbw Vale was less suited to the needs of a modern iron and steel industry. Read *Connections* 45 Activity 2, and then study map **B** and photo **C** opposite. Explain why, by the 1950s, the site had disadvantages for a modern steel industry.

4 a) Using box **B** and matrix **D** on *Connections* 45, together with map **D** and photo **E** above, give Llanwern a score for its site.
b) Give four reasons, with examples from map **D** and photo **E**, why Llanwern was a good site for a modern steelworks (use *Connections* 37 diagram **C** as a guide).

5 Draw annotated sketch maps of i) Ebbw Vale ii) Llanwern, labelling the site factors that led to the development of the iron and steel industry at each location. On your sketch map of Ebbw Vale, label in a different colour the site factors that led to the decline of the industry by the 1960s.

What is the geographical distribution of one type of secondary activity?

Increasingly since the Second World War, it has been human and economic factors that have determined the location and distribution of such industries as car assembly. Today the three most important factors are likely to be nearness to a large market, the availability of skilled labour, and government policies (figure **A** page 68).

The graph in figure **A** below shows that very few cars – under 5 million – were produced world-wide in 1950. The map shows that nearly all of those cars – over 84 out of every 100 – came from the USA, and that most of the remainder came from either Canada or the more industrialised countries of Europe. This distribution was mainly due to the presence of raw materials (e.g. steel) and, by world standards, a large, skilled and well-paid labour force.

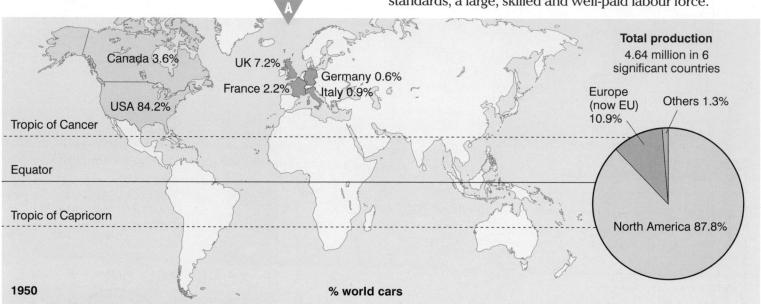

A

Canada 3.6%
UK 7.2%
Germany 0.6%
France 2.2%
Italy 0.9%
USA 84.2%

Tropic of Cancer

Equator

Tropic of Capricorn

1950   % world cars

Total production
4.64 million in 6 significant countries

Europe (now EU) 10.9%
Others 1.3%
North America 87.8%

By 1970, the number of cars produced had risen to just over 25.5 million (figure **B**). Although production was still concentrated in North America (but its share had decreased) and Western Europe (whose share had increased), cars were also being produced:

- in rapidly growing numbers in Japan as it became increasingly industrialised and wealthy

- in Mexico and Brazil which, with large internal markets, were the first two developing countries to become industrialised
- in southern hemisphere countries well away from the traditional producing areas.

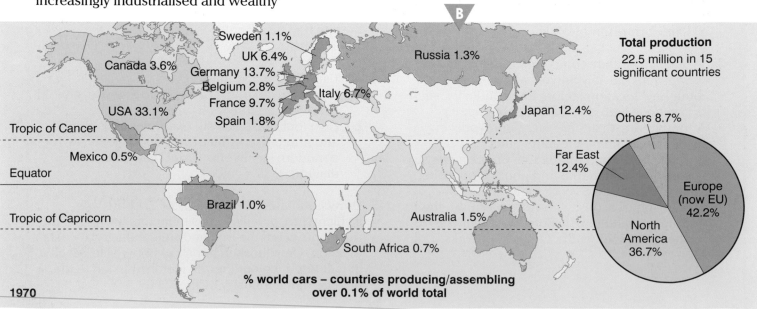

B

Sweden 1.1%
UK 6.4%
Canada 3.6%
Germany 13.7%
Belgium 2.8%
France 9.7%
USA 33.1%
Spain 1.8%
Italy 6.7%
Russia 1.3%
Japan 12.4%

Tropic of Cancer

Mexico 0.5%
Equator

Brazil 1.0%
Tropic of Capricorn
Australia 1.5%
South Africa 0.7%

1970   % world cars – countries producing/assembling over 0.1% of world total

Total production
22.5 million in 15 significant countries

Others 8.7%
Far East 12.4%
Europe (now EU) 42.2%
North America 36.7%

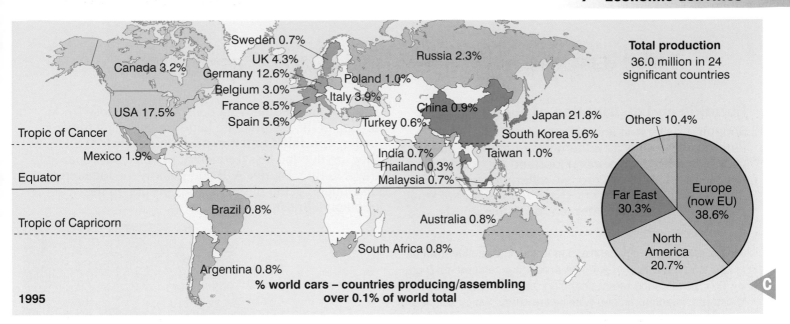

Sweden 0.7%
UK 4.3%
Canada 3.2%
Germany 12.6%
Belgium 3.0%
Poland 1.0%
Russia 2.3%
France 8.5%
Italy 3.9%
China 0.9%
USA 17.5%
Spain 5.6%
Turkey 0.6%
Japan 21.8%
South Korea 5.6%
Tropic of Cancer
Mexico 1.9%
India 0.7%
Taiwan 1.0%
Thailand 0.3%
Equator
Malaysia 0.7%
Brazil 0.8%
Australia 0.8%
Tropic of Capricorn
South Africa 0.8%
Argentina 0.8%
% world cars – countries producing/assembling over 0.1% of world total
1995

Total production
36.0 million in 24 significant countries

Others 10.4%
Far East 30.3%
Europe (now EU) 38.6%
North America 20.7%

Since 1990, when 35.7 million cars were produced, production has slowed, to 36 million in 1995 (graph in figure **C**). Production increased most rapidly in eastern Asia where one in three cars are now assembled, and decreased in North America and Western Europe. Countries such as South Korea and Malaysia (Chapter 12) have large workforces which have become increasingly skilled and who are prepared to work for lower pay than

their counterparts in Japan, North America and Europe. What the map in figure **C** does not show, however, is that car production is now dominated by several large **transnational**, or **multinational**, **companies**. A transnational company is one, like Ford, Toyota and Volkswagen, that has factories in several countries and which operates across national boundaries.

Activities

1 a) Describe the location and distribution of car-producing countries in 1950.
b) How had this location and distribution changed by: i) 1970 ii) 1995?

Car production

Rank order	1950	1970	1995
1	USA		
2	UK		
3			
4			
5			
6			
7			
8			

2 a) Make a larger copy of table **D**. Complete it by:
  i) naming the countries, in rank order of production, for each of the three years shown on the maps in figures **A**, **B** and **C**
  ii) adding colours (using the same ones as in the figures) to show the location of those countries you have named.
b) With reference to graph **E**:
  i) describe the trend (or shape) of the graphs for North America, Europe (the present EU) and the Far East
  ii) give reasons for the trend (shape) of each of the three places.

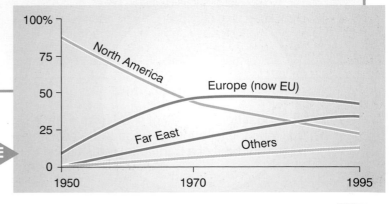

What is the geographical distribution of one type of tertiary activity?

Location and distribution of shops

Shopping, as it provides a service, is an example of a tertiary activity. Just as settlements of different size, by providing different types of goods and services, form a hierarchy (page 58), so too can different types of shop. At the base of the hierarchy (*Foundations* 58) are small shops which sell **low order**, **convenience goods** which many people want daily and to be close by. At the top of the pyramid are large shops selling **high order**, **specialist and comparison goods** for which, as they are needed less frequently, people are prepared to travel further. Figures **A**, **B** and **C** show the location and distribution of the different types of shop in the traditional British city.

A

The CBD The city centre, due to its accessibility from all parts of the urban area and surrounding settlements (page 62), became the major shopping area. It contains department stores, superstores and nationwide shops which sell high order, specialist and comparison goods (e.g. clothes, shoes, jewellery). The shops offer a wide variety of goods and sell the large volumes of stock needed to pay the high rates and rents. The major problem within the CBD became the conflict between shoppers on the one hand, and cars, delivery lorries and buses on the other.

B

The inner city Old inner city areas were characterised by the corner shop. Corner shops sold low order, convenience goods (e.g. newspapers, bread, sweets) to people who lived in nearby streets. As they were within walking distance they became a meeting place for local residents and often remained open for long hours. Due to their small size, however, they could often only stock a limited range and volume of goods. In time they began to face increased competition from the larger shops in the CBD, and were demolished during inner city redevelopment schemes.

C

The suburban fringe As cities expanded, especially between the 1920s and the 1970s, large housing estates were built at increasing distances from the city centre. In order to save local residents having to make frequent journeys into the CBD to shop, suburban shopping parades were created. Each parade was likely to consist of several low order, convenience shops together with one or two specialist shops (butcher, baker, post office) or a small chain superstore (e.g. Spar). It was also likely to have limited car-parking facilities.

Activities

1 **a)** How do different types of shop form a 'shopping hierarchy'?
   b) Describe the location and distribution of shops in: i) the city centre (CBD) ii) the inner city
   iii) the suburbs of a traditional British town or city.

Changes in the location and distribution of shops

Towns and cities are always changing. These changes often involve the location and distribution of shops. Increasingly since the 1970s, shoppers have had increased mobility (more people own their own car), improved accessibility (better urban roads give them access to a greater range of shopping centres) and preferences to buy in bulk, to shop at times convenient to them (late at night, on Sundays) and to buy their goods under one roof at a location where car parking is provided (edge-of-city hypermarkets, regional shopping centres). Figures **D**, **E** and **F** summarise some of the more important changes in the location and distribution of shops.

The CBD   Changes in the CBD have often included attempts to reduce traffic congestion and to improve the safety and comfort of shoppers. Reducing traffic congestion has been achieved either by closing off streets completely to all traffic and making them pedestrianised, or limiting vehicle access to delivery lorries (and then perhaps only at certain times of the day) and/or buses. While such schemes make shopping both safer and cleaner, the construction of covered shopping malls protects shoppers from the weather and shortens distances between shops.

D

The inner city   Due to competition from city centre shops, many corner shops have either closed down or now specialise in ethnic or fast foods (take-aways). Where large-scale redevelopment schemes led to large-scale clearances, many sites along main roads which lead into the CBD are now occupied by DIY, furniture and carpet warehouses or by car salesrooms. The types of shop located here have in some cases moved from the city centre to take advantage of cheaper land values and to provide large volumes of stock and car-parking space.

E

The edge of cities   The biggest change in shopping location has been the development of 'out-of-town' shopping centres. These centres, which include hypermarkets and superstores, often form regional shopping centres or retail parks (MetroCentre, Meadowhall and Lakeside). The main attractions of these sites to shop-owners are the lower land values, space for large buildings and associated car parks, and the ease of delivery. The main attractions to the shopper are the availability of free parking, the large volume and wide range of stock, the opportunity to buy in bulk, and the completion of purchases under one roof.

F

2 a) What processes have caused changes in the location and distribution of shops?
  b) Describe how the types of shop have changed in: i) the city centre (CBD) ii) the inner city
     iii) on the edge of cities.
  c) Give reasons for the changes which you described in **2b)**.

How can differences in world development be recognised?

Development means growth. Growth often involves several stages which show change and, hopefully, a progressive improvement. However, development is not easy to measure. *Connections* 86 and *Places* 7 suggest that the most common and easiest method is to measure wealth. The wealth of a country is given by its **gross national product (GNP) per person**. Based on wealth, countries can be divided into two groups – those that, because they are 'rich', are said to be **economically more developed** and those that, because they are poorer, are said to be **economically less developed** (*Places* 4–5 map **A**, *Connections* 87 map **C**). Diagram **A** shows wealth as a **topologically** transformed map. Topological maps are a simple method of showing information, and help to make easy comparisons between places. In this case, the size and shape of each country is not drawn to show its area (as is usual) but in proportion to its share of the world's GNP.

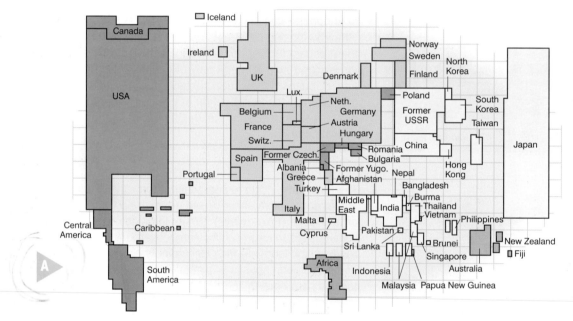

GNP is not always the most accurate method of measuring development, partly because wealth is never shared out evenly within a country or between regions. Table **B** suggests alternative ways of measuring development. Notice, however, that differences in wealth show in a country's ability to afford the basic needs of its people – food, water supply, housing, health care, education and work.

During the 1990s, the UN devised its own measure of human well-being – the **Human Development Index (HDI)**. The HDI is a social welfare index based upon education (adult literacy), health (life expectancy) and the actual purchasing power of income (economy) – see map **C**. Even so, those countries with the highest HDI (over 0.9) correspond closely with those that are economically more developed, and those with the lowest score (under 0.25) with the economically less developed.

B		
Population measure	*Conns 6, Places 8–9, Extens 44–45*	Birth rate. Death rate. Natural increase. Infant mortality. Life expectancy
Health and education	*Conns 86, Places 10–11*	Adult literacy. People per doctor or hospital bed. Diet (calories)
Work (jobs)	*Conns 86, Inter. 86, Places 10–11*	Primary, secondary, tertiary
Transport and trade	*Conns 86, Inter. 88, Places 10–11, Extens 82*	Type and km of road/rail. Primary products or manufactured goods
Energy	*Places 10–11*	Consumption per person
Material possessions	*Places 11*	e.g. cars, TVs/telephones per 1,000 people

HDI
- 0.90 and over (32 countries)
- 0.75–0.899 (32 countries)
- 0.5–0.749 (33 countries)
- 0.25–0.049 (30 countries)
- 0.048–0.249 (31 countries)

Activities

1 a) What is GNP and how is it measured?
   b) Why is GNP not always the best measure of development?

2 Compare diagram **A** with a conventional political map (map **C**).
   a) Name:
   - one country with a large area and a large proportion of the world's GNP
   - two countries with a small area but a large proportion of the world's GNP
   - two countries with a large area but a small proportion of the world's GNP.
   b) What do you notice about the size of the world's continents according to their share of the world's GNP?

3 With reference to table **B** and diagram **D**:
   a) Name three countries likely to be in the
   i) top 20 per cent   ii) bottom 20 per cent
   iii) middle 60 per cent.
   b) Apart from GNP and trade, describe eight differences in development between the top 20 per cent and bottom 20 per cent.

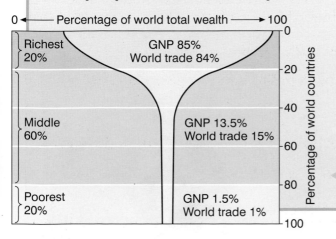

0 ← Percentage of world total wealth → 100

Richest 20%	GNP 85% World trade 84%
Middle 60%	GNP 13.5% World trade 15%
Poorest 20%	GNP 1.5% World trade 1%

Percentage of world countries — 0, 20, 40, 60, 80, 100

D

ICT Enquiry

Further your investigations into measuring development by collecting your own data. You can research statistical information from an atlas, *Philip's Geographical Digest*, a CD-ROM, a computer atlas or the Internet. For the last, the UN CyberSchoolBus (web site http://www.un.org/Pubs/CyberSchoolBus) provides an easy-to-use database with over 30 different fields of information on 185 different countries. From the UN CyberSchoolBus homepage select Resource Source, and then InfoNation.

Stages in your enquiry Select 10 countries (perhaps using *Places* 4–5 map **A**) – five from the richer, more developed North and five from the poorer, less developed South. Select 10 indicators (taken from *Connections*, *Interactions* and *Places*) to investigate each country.

Conducting your research Use one or more of the sources listed above.

Presenting your results You could do this either as a table (see *Places* 11 table **D**), by producing graphs for each indicator using a graph package on your CD-ROM, or by producing spreadsheets and charts.

Writing up your results Describe and explain what you have discovered about your 10 countries. You could use a word-processor for this, inserting your graphs into your word-processing file.

Conclusion Produce a rank order list for your 10 countries according to their level of development. Write a paragraph outlining the characteristics of different levels of development.

4 a) What is the HDI? How is it different from GNP?
   b) Describe the global location of countries with the highest HDI (over 0.9) and those with the lowest HDI (under 0.25).

How do differences in development affect the quality of life of different groups of people?

The term **sustainable development** has been used by geographers for over a decade and more recently by politicians. Like development, it is a difficult term to define. Ideally it should lead to an improvement in people's:

- **standard of living** – enabling them, and future generations, to become better off financially (economically)

- **quality of life** – allowing them to become more content with their way of life and the environment in which they live.

This may be achieved in a variety of ways. These are summarised in figure **A** and explained in more detail in *Places* 56 figure **A**.

Develop materials and utensils that will use fewer resources and last longer.

Develop technology appropriate to the skills, wealth and needs of local people and develop local skills so that they may be passed on to future generations.

Use natural resources in a way (renew, recycle and replace) that will not spoil the environment (landscape and wildlife).

Allow the economic development of a country at a pace it can afford (so that it does not fall into debt).

Many people, especially in economically developed countries, have several misconceptions regarding development. One is a belief that standard of living and quality of life mean the same thing, and that one cannot be achieved without the other. Diagrams **B** to **E** look at the lifestyles of four groups of people living in different parts of the world.

We live in a clearing in the Amazon rainforest (*Places* 26). The clearing was made by cutting down just sufficient trees for our communal house and the small area needed to grow crops. Each day the men go hunting and fishing while the women do the washing, look after the crops and prepare the meals. Although we only grow enough for our own needs, the soil soon becomes infertile and after a few years we have to move so that the soil and the forest can recover. We use very few resources and, although we occasionally exchange goods with neighbouring tribes, have very little contact with the outside world. We live as best as we can in harmony with our environment.

We have just retired. We have bought our own house in a quiet village only 20 km from a town that has good shops and places of entertainment. We still garden quite a lot but we have plenty of time to relax in the evenings, to join in village events and to visit or receive our family and friends. As we both had good, though not highly-paid jobs, we managed to save enough money which now allows us to take a holiday each summer and to rent an apartment in Spain for several months during the winter.

We are refugees. We were forced to leave our homes and our few possessions last year due to a severe drought which ruined our crops and left us without food. This year the camp has become very crowded as more people have been forced to move, partly because of the continued drought and partly due to civil war. Many of our friends died on their way to the camp due to exhaustion and a lack of food, and others have died since they arrived. At present we get one meal a day but food is running out and there are virtually no medical supplies left for the many people who are seriously ill and undernourished.

D

We live in a large house 60 km from central London. We have very highly-paid jobs in the City of London. We need the high salaries to pay for the mortgage on our house, the loans on our two cars and the journey to work. Commuting takes up to two hours each way. Driving is impossible due to congestion and the high cost of parking. Instead we catch a crowded train to London and then, if it is raining, an equally crowded tube train or, if it is dry, we walk past people who are homeless and begging and along roads full of vehicle fumes and rubbish. We get home tired, and late, most evenings, but we enjoy being out of the city at weekends.

E

Activities

1 a) What is meant by the term **sustainable development**?

b) What is the difference between **standard of living** and **quality of life**?

c) How, according to figure **A**, can sustainable development be achieved?

2 a) Figures **B** to **E** refer to four groups of people living in different parts of the world. Which group has:

i) the highest standard of living and the highest quality of life

ii) the highest standard of living and the lowest quality of life

iii) the lowest standard of living and the highest quality of life

iv) the lowest standard of living and the lowest quality of life?

b) Give reasons for each of your answers in **a)**.

3 Standard of living and quality of life can vary within countries and within cities as well as between countries.

i) Maria and Roberto (figure **F**) live in São Paulo. The differences in their way of life are described in *Places* 24–25.

ii) Kip, Krista, Julius and Marietta (figure **A**) live in Nairobi. The differences in their way of life are described in *Places* 48–49.

For *either* i) *or* ii) describe and give reasons for the differences in their standard of living and quality of life.

F

World citizenship – how can the more fortunate help the less fortunate?

One way of trying to help countries to develop and improve their standard of living and quality of life is to provide them with **aid**. Aid is a term used to describe any type of help given to a country. It can range from technical equipment and money to skilled workers and emergency supplies.

Most aid is given by governments of rich countries, either directly or through international organisations, to poorer countries, mainly in Africa, Asia and Latin America (table **A**). Often, however, the most effective aid is provided by voluntary organisations (figures **B** and **C**). Poorer countries may need aid:

- to help them develop their economies so that they can increase their share of world trade and improve their standard of living
- to provide basic services and amenities such as a reliable water supply, hospitals and schools which help raise their quality of life
- following disasters which may either be natural, such as flooding (figure **E**) and earthquakes (page 8), or human-induced, such as civil war
- to help preserve their environment.

	Type of aid
Bilateral	**Government to government/rich country to poor country** **Advantages** include: large amounts can benefit large numbers of people; can develop a poor country's industry, public services and economic growth; can increase economic and political stability. **Disadvantages** include: often 'strings' attached which tie the poor country to the rich country, i.e. has to buy goods from rich country. The poorer country often falls further into debt. Within the developing country, little wealth is passed down to the poor, especially in rural areas. It does not always encourage self-help.
Multilateral	Rich governments contribute to international organisations like the United Nations Children's Fund (UNICEF), the World Bank and the EU Development Fund. Meant to be no ties, but increasingly there are.
Non-governmental organisations (voluntary)	Aid from charities, churches and other groups such as Oxfam, Christian Aid, ActionAid and Intermediate Technology. It can be: **short-term** – following disasters like flooding, earthquakes and hurricanes **long-term** – development projects working with local communities; projects are often small and sustainable, less financial support but more effective.

Learning skills at a training centre for teenage girls in Bangladesh

ActionAid exists to help overcome poverty and improve the quality of life in the developing world. The organisation works directly with three million of the poorest children, families and communities throughout Africa, Asia and Latin America. ActionAid is one of the UK's largest development charities.

How can just £2 a month help poor people to help themselves?

These days, £2 won't buy very much. But if you give £2 a month to Oxfam, your donation is stretched much further. We support people who are helping themselves, so they contribute their hard work, their time and energy to make every penny go further.

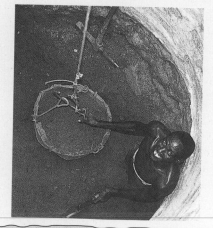

Train 2 voluntary health workers

In India, £2 a month will help pay and train 2 voluntary health workers, safeguarding *hundreds* of people.

Clean water for a whole community

In Sudan, £2 a month will help provide enough tools for villagers to dig a well and give a permanent supply of clean, safe water.

Plant 670 trees

Your £2 a month could supply 670 seedlings every year, which will be planted out by local Ethiopian farmers.

Source: Oxfam, October 1998

Activities

1 a) What is meant by the term **aid**?

b) What is the difference between bilateral, multilateral and non-governmental organisation aid?

c) What are the advantages and disadvantages of bilateral aid?

d) How do organisations such as ActionAid (figure **B**) and Oxfam (figure **C**) help people living in developing countries?

2 Deciding how to spend money allocated as aid involves making difficult choices. Imagine you are an aid worker in a poor country. You are given two donations, one for £24 a year (figure **C**), the other for £20 million (figure **D**). In each case you are given options as to how you might spend the money. Explain, with reasons, your decision.

3 a) As part of your investigation of aid, you have to find out about various aid organisations and their campaigns. With reference to figure **E**:

i) How is the advertisement suggesting that you can help?

ii) Is the advertisement successful in making you want to help? Explain your answer.

b) You could investigate how various organisations try to i) collect donations ii) help people in poorer countries by writing off for leaflets, collecting adverts in newspapers or received in your post, or visiting web sites. The following web sites will provide you with a good start:

- One World Online is a partnership of over 100 organisations working for human rights and sustainable development:

   http://www.oneworld.org/

- Oxfam UK Homepage:

   http://www.oxfam.org.uk/

- Christian Aid UK Homepage:

   http://www.christian-aid.org.uk

- Intermediate Technology:

   http://www.oneworld.org/itdg

c) Your class could support an aid campaign in school, perhaps by using information that you discovered while working on this topic. You might:

i) make a presentation to your year-group in a school assembly outlining ways your school could help the aid organisation

ii) design campaign posters and leaflets using a DTP program.

D

How can aid be spent?
Here are some of the ways that £20 million could be spent:

- immunise 2 million children against the six main preventable diseases
- provide basic village-level water supplies to one million people
- fund slum-improvement projects for over 100,000 families
- build between 350 and 3,500 km of rural access roads.

Source: ActionAid

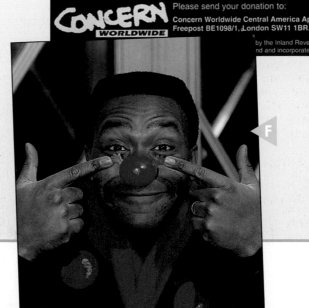

CRISIS IN CENTRAL AMERICA

E

In the aftermath of Hurricane Mitch the facts speak for themselves...

- **As many as 9,000 dead**
- **More than 15,000 missing**
- **Over 2 million homeless**
- **80% of crops wiped out**
- **Typhoid, cholera, malaria and dengue threaten thousands of lives**

Without waiting for outside help, local communities have sprung into action to provide assistance to those left destitute. However, they lack even the basics such as clean water, food, shelter materials and medicine and this is why we are asking for your help.

Concern Worldwide's emergency team will be working through local partners to provide medical equipment and shelter material to those who need it most.

Please send a gift today and help support our emergency work in Central America.

Photo: Associated Press

CONCERN WORLDWIDE

Please send your donation to:
Concern Worldwide Central America Appeal, Freepost BE1098/1, London SW11 1BR.

by the Inland Revenue
nd and incorporated in NI.

F

How does the interdependence of countries affect development?

All countries want to be independent, both politically and economically. Independence means that a country can make its own decisions as to how to develop and how its people should live. In reality, no country can be completely independent as it is unlikely to have all the raw materials (natural resources), manufactured goods and services that it needs. As a result countries have either to work together or rely on each other, a process known as **interdependence**.

Most countries become interdependent through **trade**. Trade is when one country buys (**imports**) or sells (**exports**) goods to another country. Goods can be classified as being **primary** or **manufactured**.

- **Primary** goods are raw materials such as foodstuffs (tea, coffee, wheat), minerals (tin, copper) and timber. Primary goods are usually low in value.

- **Manufactured** goods (page 66) include cars, machinery and electrical goods. Manufactured goods are higher in value.

Most economically developing countries (many of which are former colonies) have to rely upon the sale of primary goods. Most economically developed countries (many of which are former colonial powers) rely upon selling manufactured goods (diagram **A**). This means that the developing countries are likely to remain poor while the developed countries become richer. In time, the developing country will have to ask the developed country for **aid** (page 80 and *Interactions* 90).

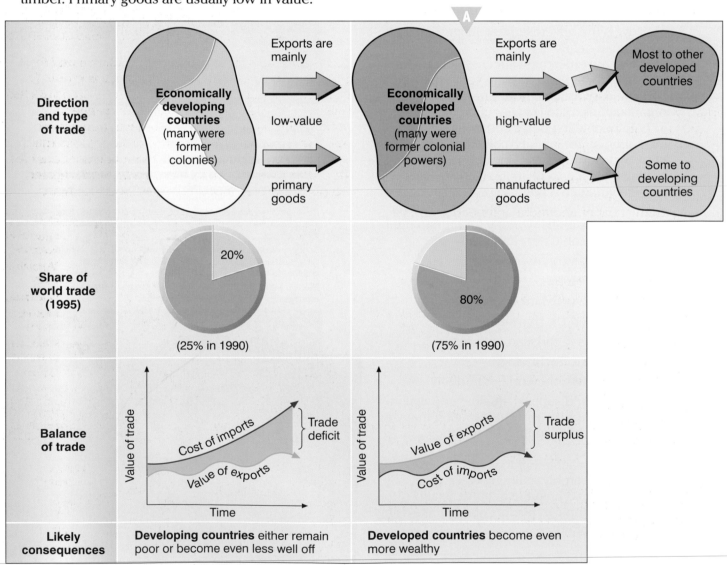

A

Direction and type of trade	Economically developing countries (many were former colonies) → Exports are mainly low-value primary goods	Economically developed countries (many were former colonial powers) → Exports are mainly high-value manufactured goods → Most to other developed countries / Some to developing countries
Share of world trade (1995)	20% (25% in 1990)	80% (75% in 1990)
Balance of trade	Value of trade — Cost of imports, Value of exports — Trade deficit — Time	Value of trade — Value of exports, Cost of imports — Trade surplus — Time
Likely consequences	**Developing countries** either remain poor or become even less well off	**Developed countries** become even more wealthy

Developing countries are faced with two further problems.

1 Many of them have to rely, for their exports, upon just one or two items (*Interactions* 89). If this is a crop that fails or a mineral that sees a fall in international prices, then the country will receive even less income.

2 International prices in primary goods tend to go up and down, whereas those of manufactured goods are more likely to show a more even and steady rise (see graphs at bottom of diagram **A**). Economic planning is more difficult in countries where income is less reliable.

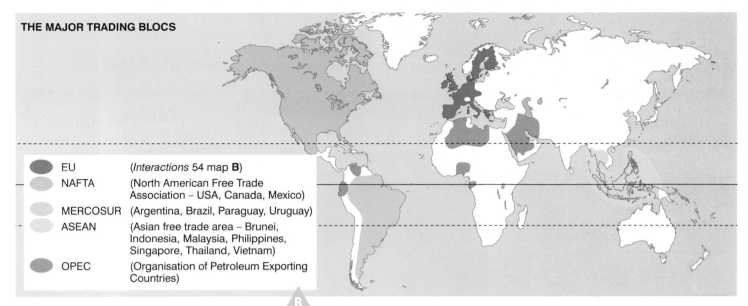

THE MAJOR TRADING BLOCS

EU	(*Interactions* 54 map **B**)	
NAFTA	(North American Free Trade Association – USA, Canada, Mexico)	
MERCOSUR	(Argentina, Brazil, Paraguay, Uruguay)	
ASEAN	(Asian free trade area – Brunei, Indonesia, Malaysia, Philippines, Singapore, Thailand, Vietnam)	
OPEC	(Organisation of Petroleum Exporting Countries)	

B

Trading blocs

In an attempt to increase their trade, many countries have grouped together to form **trading blocs** (map **B**). The UK is one of the 15 members of the second largest trading bloc, the European Union (EU). Within the EU there is a single market. This has been achieved by eliminating customs duties, known as **tariffs**, that were previously paid on goods moving between member countries. This lowered the price of imported goods, making them cheaper and more competitive against

goods from non-EU countries such as Japan and the USA. Also, as the size of the EU market has grown (it now has a population of 375 million compared with 395 million in NAFTA) then so too has the number of potential customers. Trading blocs can also impose restrictions, or **trade barriers**, to protect goods made by their member states against those of other countries. This action, which restricts **free trade**, works against the poorer, economically less developed countries.

Activities

1 Diagram **C** and *Places* 58–59, 106–107 will help you to answer this question.
   a) Which items shown in the key of diagram **C** are
      i) primary goods   ii) manufactured goods?
   b) What are the main differences in exports between Kenya and Japan?
   c) What are the main differences in imports between Kenya and Japan?
   d) From your answers to **b)** and **c)**, explain why Kenya's trade is more typical of an economically developing country and Japan more typical of an economically developed country.

2 Diagram **D** shows the balance of trade for two countries. Which is likely to be the economically developing country and which the economically developed country? Give reasons for your answer.

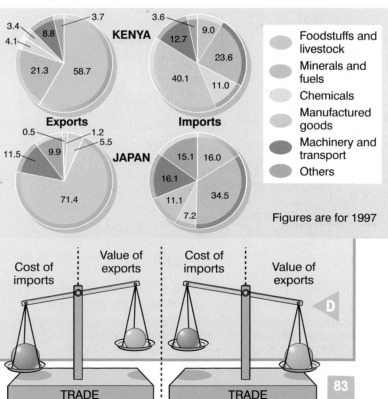

KENYA

3.4
4.1
8.8
3.7
21.3
58.7

3.6
9.0
12.7
23.6
40.1
11.0

Exports   **Imports**

JAPAN

0.5
1.2
5.5
11.5
9.9
71.4

15.1
16.0
16.1
34.5
11.1
7.2

	Foodstuffs and livestock
	Minerals and fuels
	Chemicals
	Manufactured goods
	Machinery and transport
	Others

Figures are for 1997

C

Cost of imports — Value of exports | Cost of imports — Value of exports

TRADE   TRADE

D

How can conflicts arise in areas of scenic attraction?

We all have different ideas about what is attractive, whether it is clothes, music or, in this case, scenery. By scenic attraction, we mean places of outstanding natural beauty. These places can vary in size from the Canadian Rockies down to the English Lake District (*Interactions* 98–99), and even to individual landforms such as Niagara Falls (*Connections* 11). Scenic areas often owe their attractiveness to tectonic, river, coastal or glacial processes (figure **A**). Their beauty may be further enhanced by natural vegetation and exotic plants.

A

Tectonic scenery

Forms high mountains (Alps and Rockies). Both active (Hawaii) and extinct (Mt Fuji) volcanoes.

River scenery

Waterfalls (Niagara, Victoria and Iguaçu Falls). Deep gorges. Rivers themselves attract people.

Glaciated scenery

Spectacular peaks (Matterhorn) and ridges (Striding Edge). Many lakes (Lake District) and waterfalls. Glaciers.

Coastal scenery

Headlands and high cliffs. Sandy bays. Narrow inlets. Fjords (Norway).

Vegetated scenery

Abundance of vegetation in rainforest. Autumn (Fall) in the USA.

In recent years an increasing number of people have been attracted to scenic areas in many parts of the world. This is partly due to improvements in transport, making even remote places more accessible, and increases in wealth and leisure time (*Interactions* 40).

It is also due to people seeing distant places on the TV and reading about them in travel magazines. However, the increasing number of visitors to scenic areas causes conflict within those places (diagram **B**). Conflicts may be between:

- Different types of land users such as farmers, water authorities, quarrying firms and the Ministry of Defence
- people who live and work in scenic areas and tourists who visit them
- different groups of tourists, including those who want to relax and enjoy the peace, wildlife and scenery, and those who want to be active and, for example, ski or take part in water sports.

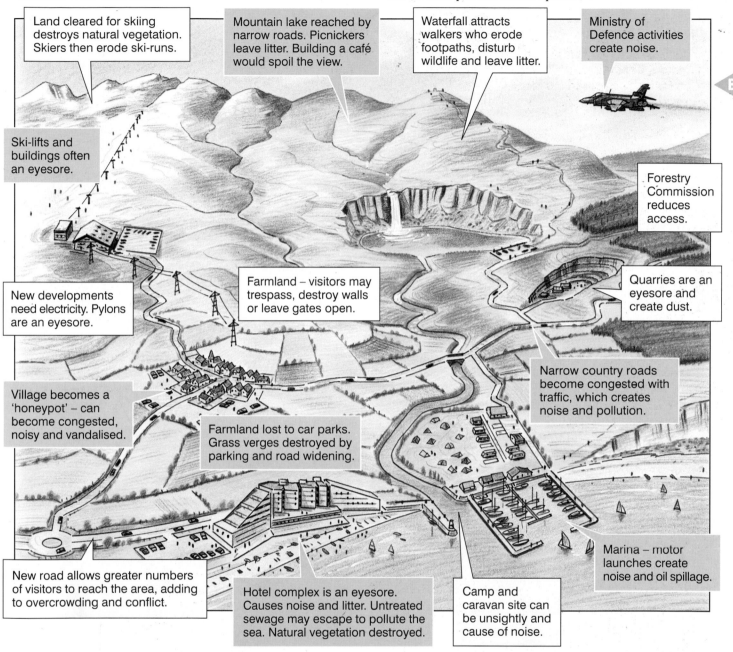

Land cleared for skiing destroys natural vegetation. Skiers then erode ski-runs.

Mountain lake reached by narrow roads. Picnickers leave litter. Building a café would spoil the view.

Waterfall attracts walkers who erode footpaths, disturb wildlife and leave litter.

Ministry of Defence activities create noise.

Ski-lifts and buildings often an eyesore.

Forestry Commission reduces access.

New developments need electricity. Pylons are an eyesore.

Farmland – visitors may trespass, destroy walls or leave gates open.

Quarries are an eyesore and create dust.

Village becomes a 'honeypot' – can become congested, noisy and vandalised.

Narrow country roads become congested with traffic, which creates noise and pollution.

Farmland lost to car parks. Grass verges destroyed by parking and road widening.

New road allows greater numbers of visitors to reach the area, adding to overcrowding and conflict.

Hotel complex is an eyesore. Causes noise and litter. Untreated sewage may escape to pollute the sea. Natural vegetation destroyed.

Camp and caravan site can be unsightly and cause of noise.

Marina – motor launches create noise and oil spillage.

B

Activities

1 a) Name three areas which, in your opinion, are the most scenically attractive that you have visited.
   b) Why did you find each of them attractive?
   c) Name five scenically attractive areas that you would like to visit. Locate each area and explain why you would like to visit it. (You may need to refer to travel brochures to help select the areas.)

2 a) Between which groups of people are conflicts likely to occur in areas of scenic attraction?
   b) Using figure B, describe how increasing numbers of visitors can affect: i) the natural scenery ii) vegetation and wildlife iii) the way of live of local residents.

What attempts have been made to manage areas of scenic attraction?

During the 1940s in the UK there was growing concern over the increased number of people, and vehicles, visiting areas of scenic attraction. It became obvious that if attempts were not made to manage and protect certain areas then the environment in these places could be permanently damaged. The result was the creation, by an Act of Parliament, of ten National Parks in England and Wales (*Interactions* 43 figure **C**) and ten Authorities to look after them (figure **A**). The main aims of National Parks are summarised in figure **B**.

A

National Parks were defined as 'areas of great natural beauty which give opportunities for open-air recreation, established so that their natural beauty can be preserved and enhanced, and so that the enjoyment of the scenery by the public can be promoted'.

B

Each National Park Authority has to:

- protect and enhance the landscape (photo **C**)

- help the public to relax, and to encourage them to take part in outdoor recreational activities

- protect the social and economic well-being of people who live and/or work in the National Park (photo **D**).

Some of the ways in which the National Parks Authorities have achieved these aims are shown in *Interactions* 42 figure **A**. Although National Parks can now be found in most parts of the world, they are not the only method of protecting scenic areas and their wildlife. Other methods include nature reserves (grid reference 990862 on the OS map page 55), game reserves (*Places* 44) and marine reserves.

Unfortunately, attempts to protect and manage areas of scenic attraction do not always prove to be as successful as was first planned. For example, the creation of the Yellowstone (the world's first), Yosemite and Grand Canyon National Parks in western USA has had, in parts and unintentionally, several adverse effects (figure **E**).

C

D

Case Study

Yellowstone, Yosemite and Grand Canyon National Parks
National Parks in America protect areas of wilderness. Unlike those in Western Europe, little of the land in these Parks had been farmed or put to other use. Within the Parks, the conservation of wildlife is considered to be as important as the protection of the scenery. The construction of new all-weather highways and the building of holiday lodges, tourist villages and motels has encouraged an increasing number of city-dwelling Americans to enjoy 'the great outdoors'.

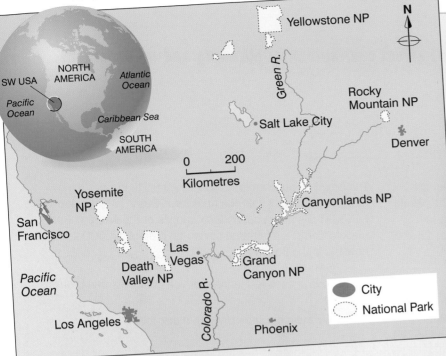

The Grand Canyon National Park

The National Parks in the west of America (figure **E**) include Yellowstone (noted for its geysers, hot springs, bears, buffalo and elk), Yosemite (with its waterfalls), and the Grand Canyon (where the Colorado River, ideal for whitewater rafting, has cut a gorge almost 2 km deep). However, over 30 million people live within 500 km of these National Parks. Add to this the considerable number of overseas tourists and you can see why each of these three Parks has more than 5 million visitors a year and why the more famous locations (**honeypots**) are under pressure. Some of the unintentional effects caused by the large number of visitors include the following:

- The best viewing points are soon filled and people have to queue, for example to see the Old Faithful geyser which erupts about every 85 minutes (figure **E**).
- Car parks and holiday accommodation are often filled by mid-morning.
- The bears, a major attraction in Yellowstone, have retreated to the more remote parts of the Park.
- The Grand Canyon attracts so many rafters and canoeists that it can take several years for a private party to obtain a permit to travel through it.
- Small frontier settlements on the edges of the Parks are growing into large tourist and retirement centres.

Yosemite National Park

Old Faithful, Yellowstone National Park

Activities

1 a) Why were National Parks created in England and Wales?
   b) What are the main aims of the National Park Authorities?

2 a) What are the natural advantages which attract so many people to the Yellowstone, Yosemite and Grand Canyon National Parks?
   b) Give three reasons why pressure on these Parks has increased in recent years.
   c) Describe some of the unintentional effects which have resulted from attempts to plan and manage these Parks.

How does sustainable development affect environmental planning and management?

Case Study

Tropical rainforests

The characteristic features of the tropical rainforest are described on pages 38–39 and *Interactions* 10–11. While reading these extracts you may have also studied the influence of human activity on the rainforest (*Places* 28–29) and considered whether its development could be sustainable (*Places* 36–37).

Photos **A** and **B** are **satellite images** showing part of Rondonia, a state in the south-west of the Amazon Basin in Brazil, where there has been considerable deforestation of the rainforest. These images were taken from the Earthshots USGS Internet web site:

http://edcwww.cr.usgs.gov/earthshots/fast/Rondonia/

The Brazilian government also uses satellite images to monitor changes within the rainforest. Every 16 days, the LANDSAT 5 satellite sends 229 images of the Amazon Basin back to Earth. Each image covers an area of 34,000 km^2 (so how big is the Basin?).

If you have access to the Internet you could visit the project's web site:

http://www.dpi.inpe.br/grid/quick-looks

A — 1975

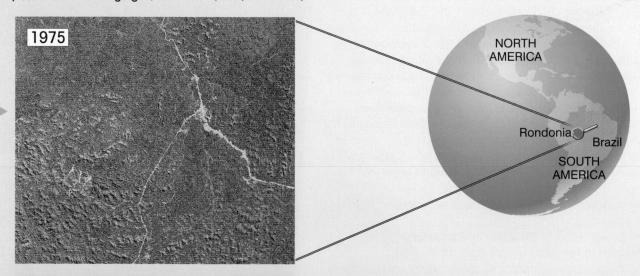

Notice how, on the satellite images, systematic cutting of the vegetation starts alongside roads and then fans out to create a 'feather' or 'fishbone' pattern. The deforested land and urban areas appear in light blue; healthy vegetation appears red.

The tropical rainforest is being cleared indiscriminately at an alarming rate, mainly by large transnational (multinational) corporations. In contrast, many governments and environmental organisations now believe that future developments must be sustainable. Three examples of sustainable schemes are outlined in figures **C**, **D** and **E**.

B — 1992

Brazil launches ambitious plan to save rainforest

29 April 1998

Up to 62 million acres of threatened Amazon rainforest would be preserved under a program unveiled on Wednesday by the Brazilian government.

President Fernando Henrique Cardoso said his country – in cooperation with the World Bank and the Worldwide Fund for Nature – would protect 10 percent of its forests by the year 2000.

The cost of the project – which would set aside an area the size of Britain – is estimated at between $84 million and $156 million, much of which will come from the World Bank.

Source: CNN News

Amazonian Vines: a Feasible Forest Product

The Amazon is an ideal source for providing a reliable supply of rattan-like vines and other natural fibres. Studies indicate that many of these species can be cultivated and managed within forests, allowing a sustainable, high-volume supply of materials. Currently most of the Amazonian vines used in the Brazilian wicker industry are collected wild. The Liana Project will develop industries which will:1 cultivate and collect these vines in a sustainable, ecologically sensitive manner, 2 locally add value to vines by producing finished goods and semi-finished products. Hopefully this will provide an economically viable alternative to unsustainable deforestation for short-term gain.

Source: Rainforest Action Network

Brazil hopes new push for ecotourism can help save Amazon rainforest

28 January 1998

More than 10 million people live in Brazil's Amazon jungle, and many of them rely on the riches of the forest to survive, leading to deforestation of an area the size of France, since the 1970s. Though the Brazilian government has tried to crack down on deforestation, the destruction accelerates. Inhabitants of the Amazon say it's a matter of survival. The area is so vast that it's virtually impossible to control deforestation by force. So the government is trying a different tactic: ecotourism – spending millions to develop tourism centred on nature. 'People can make money from the rainforest without destroying it,' said Aldenir Paraguassu of Brazil's Environment Ministry. 'It's just a matter of showing them how,' with strategies like conferences and educational material. The jungle is already attracting tourists from around the world. Tourists hire local guides to learn about the rainforest and to journey upriver, where they visit remote villages and buy handicrafts made by those who live there. They stay at hotels which range from luxurious to primitive – like a jungle lodge, built literally in the trees, hours from civilization. The ecotourism boom has created hundreds of new jobs and put money in the pockets of local residents. 'Those involved in ecotourism are now looking at the rainforest differently,' environmentalist Alcide Filho said. 'It is the reason visitors are here spending money.'

Source: CNN News

Activities

1 a) Look carefully at the two satellite images **A** and **B**. Describe and explain the differences between them (page 39, and *Places* 28–29 should help you with your answer).

   b) Why do you think that the Brazilian government uses satellite images to monitor environmental change in the Amazon rainforest?

   c) If you have access to the Internet you could visit the Earthshots web site, copy and paste the images into a desktop publishing program, and label the changes using the software tools.

2 a) Explain how the three schemes described in figures **C**, **D** and **E** represent examples of sustainable development.

   b) Try to find other examples of sustainable development from around the world. You could refer to:

   i) pages 86 and 95, *Interactions* 91, *Places* 56–57, 104–105

   ii) the Internet, e.g. web sites:
   Rainforest Action Network
   http://www.ran.org/
   Worldwide Fund for Nature
   http://www.panda.org

What are the problems in providing a reliable supply of fresh water?

A reliable supply of fresh water is essential for all forms of life on Earth. A glance at a world map shows that as over 70 per cent of the Earth's surface is covered by seas and oceans, there should be sufficient water for all. However, as this water is salty, it is unsuitable for human use (*Foundations* 38 diagram **A**). Added to this, much of the remainder is stored either as ice and snow, or deep underground (page 27 diagram **C**).

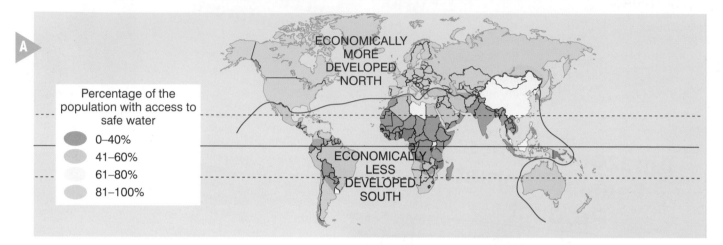

Percentage of the population with access to safe water
- 0–40%
- 41–60%
- 61–80%
- 81–100%

ECONOMICALLY MORE DEVELOPED NORTH

ECONOMICALLY LESS DEVELOPED SOUTH

Of the Earth's land surface, one-third is too dry for settlement or farming. Over another one-third, a reliable water supply is not guaranteed, especially in economically less developed countries. According to the United Nations, between 1.5 billion (30 per cent) and 2 billion (40 per cent) of the world's population lack a safe water supply (map **A**). Many other people are affected by short-term disruptions caused by drought, flooding or pollution. The result, according to UN estimates, is that each day some 25,000 people die from using contaminated water.

One-quarter of Calcutta's population of 11.6 million has no access to piped water. It is not uncommon in the poorer bustees for a single tap to be shared by 35–45 families. With few homes having toilets, sewage often runs down the narrow lanes, contaminating drinking water.

Economically developing countries

Problems of providing a reliable supply of water are most serious:
- in urban areas, especially shanty settlements, where there is
  i) a shortage of pipes to bring fresh water (figure **B**)
  ii) an absence of drains, which means that sewage may pollute water supplies (*Connections* 84–85, *Places* 25 and 49)
  iii) a rapidly growing population
- in rural areas where rivers and streams may be used for drinking, washing and the disposal of sewage, and which may be a long distance from the village
- at times of drought (as in the Sudan in 1998) and after serious flooding (figure **C**).

The 1998 floods in Bangladesh covered two-thirds of the country for over two months. During that time 30 million people were made homeless. Water supplies, even for those who previously had them, were contaminated, causing outbreaks of cholera and diarrhoea.

Economically developed countries

Most economically developed countries have:

- a more reliable supply of water although, as in the UK (*Foundations* 39) and southern California (map **D**), the water may have to be transferred from one part of the country to another

- greater wealth and technology, enabling them to build large dams – water stored in reservoirs behind the dams can be transferred when needed by a series of pipes to individual homes.

Case Study

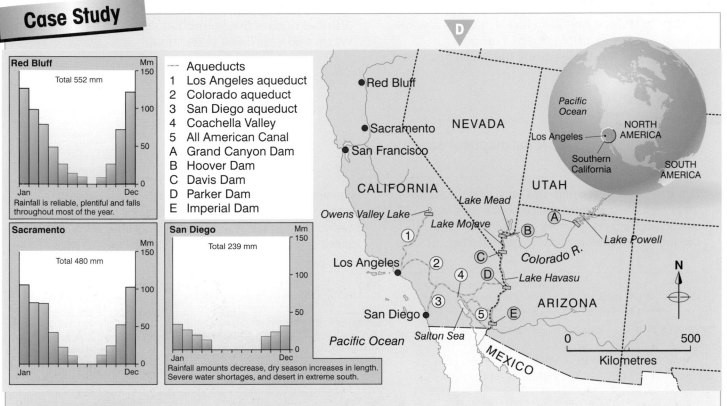

Red Bluff — Mm 150, 100, 50, 0. Total 552 mm. Jan — Dec. Rainfall is reliable, plentiful and falls throughout most of the year.

Sacramento — Mm 150, 100, 50, 0. Total 480 mm. Jan — Dec.

San Diego — Mm 150, 100, 50, 0. Total 239 mm. Jan — Dec. Rainfall amounts decrease, dry season increases in length. Severe water shortages, and desert in extreme south.

Aqueducts
1 Los Angeles aqueduct
2 Colorado aqueduct
3 San Diego aqueduct
4 Coachella Valley
5 All American Canal
A Grand Canyon Dam
B Hoover Dam
C Davis Dam
D Parker Dam
E Imperial Dam

Southern California

California's basic problem is that its **water demand** far exceeds its **water supply**. This is mainly because it is the northern parts, which are less populated, that receive most rainfall, whereas it is the more southern areas, where most people live, that receive least rainfall (map **A**). Many people have been attracted to Los Angeles (12.4 million) and San Diego (2.6 million) because of their sunshine. However, the near-desert climate means that water has to be brought considerable distances (map **D**). Large dams on the Colorado River, which prevent flooding and help generate hydro-electricity, have created huge lakes, some of which are used as reservoirs. Water from the Colorado River is taken by the Colorado aqueduct for domestic and industrial use in Los Angeles and San Diego, and by the Coachella and All American Canal for farming around the inland Salton Sea (map **D**).

Activities

1 a) Why do developing countries often find it difficult to provide a reliable supply of fresh water?

   b) How, according to *Interactions* 91, may some people in developing countries obtain a reliable supply of fresh water?

   c) i) How has Egypt managed to provide a reliable supply of water for its population (*Foundations* 42–43)?

      ii) How did the provision of a reliable supply create other problems in the Nile Valley?

2 a) List five ways by which, according to *Foundations* 38, people in Britain may obtain a reliable supply of fresh water.

   b) How do the desert areas of southern California receive a reliable supply of water?

What are the causes and effects of water pollution and how may it be prevented?

Connections 16–19 investigated the causes and effects of water pollution in the River Tyne and the North Sea. You will have seen that while it is both possible and necessary to reduce pollution levels, it is not always easy to do so. For example, many European settlements and industries along the North Sea coast were used to dumping their sewage and other waste into the sea (*Connections* 18 map **A**). Pollution levels became so high that the European Union established a number of directives aimed at reducing the disposal of waste and improving water quality.

Case Study

Scarborough waste water disposal scheme

Stage 1

Construction work began in 1987 and was completed in 1991 on the first stage of a scheme to ensure that Scarborough's bathing waters complied with the EU's bathing water directive. Although this first stage, which is summarised in figure **A**, did improve the existing disposal system, it proved to be unpopular with some groups in the local community (figure **B**). The screening plant at Scalby Mills is located at grid reference 036907 on the OS map on page 55.

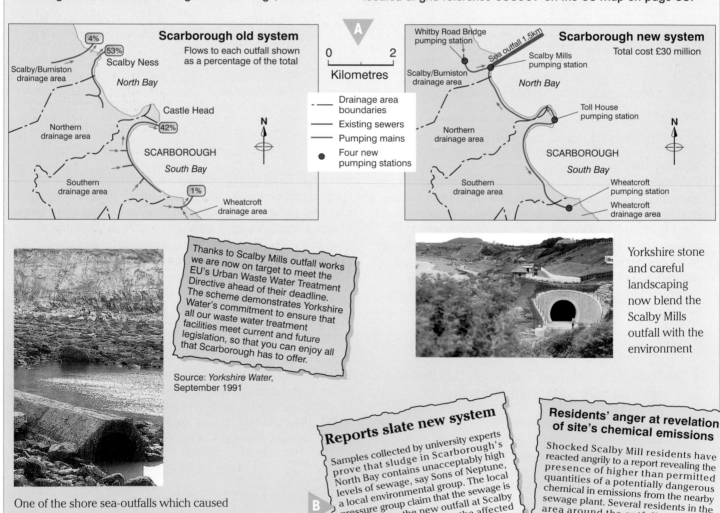

One of the shore sea-outfalls which caused problems at Scarborough before 1991

Thanks to Scalby Mills outfall works we are now on target to meet the EU's Urban Waste Water Treatment Directive ahead of their deadline. The scheme demonstrates Yorkshire Water's commitment to ensure that all our waste water treatment facilities meet current and future legislation, so that you can enjoy all that Scarborough has to offer.

Source: *Yorkshire Water*, September 1991

Yorkshire stone and careful landscaping now blend the Scalby Mills outfall with the environment

Reports slate new system

Samples collected by university experts prove that sludge in Scarborough's North Bay contains unacceptably high levels of sewage, say Sons of Neptune, a local environmental group. The local pressure group claim that the sewage is coming from the new outfall at Scalby Mills, and have called for the affected area of beach to be closed.

23 October 1991

Residents' anger at revelation of site's chemical emissions

Shocked Scalby Mill residents have reacted angrily to a report revealing the presence of higher than permitted quantities of a potentially dangerous chemical in emissions from the nearby sewage plant. Several residents in the area around the outfall plant have complained of sore throats and running eyes in recent months.

28 October 1992

Source: *Scarborough Evening News*

Stage 2

In 1997 Yorkshire Water applied for planning permission for the building of a waste water treatment works in the Scarborough area. This was to be a second phase to the 1991 development and part of a larger £120 million scheme by Yorkshire Water to upgrade sewage disposal along the east coast of the county. People in the Scarborough area generally welcomed the development which would treat waste water before it was discharged into the sea (figure **C**).

Yorkshire Water submitted two planning applications for consideration by Scarborough Council. Both sites were north of the town and both proved to be controversial. One was at Cow Wath Beck, near the village of Scalby (020913 on the OS map, page 55); the other was at Cowlam Hole, on the coast north of Scalby Lodge (027922). Figures **D** and **E** summarise the case against each site.

C ►

'Scarborough's image of a seaside resort will be strengthened with the clean-up of sewage on the east coast. Let us hope they don't take years to decide where the plant is to go. People will have to accept that it will have to go somewhere in the Scarborough area ... Nowhere is going to be perfect ... people might have to accept that it could be on their doorstep.'

Susan Ewer, President of Scarborough Hotels Association, January 1997

D ▼

Against Cow Wath Beck

Simon Lockley (below), a resident of Scalby village, was shocked when he heard of the proposals, as the Cow Wath Beck site was very close to his house. He began a local campaign protesting against the proposals, and formed a protest group called Scalby Against Sewage. The group drew people's attention to the issue by designing a logo, holding a public meeting, producing a policy statement, issuing press releases and lobbying local MPs.

Against Cowlam Hole

Both the North York Moors National Park Authority and the Countryside Commission opposed this site, which was located on the Heritage Coast. They claimed that the scheme would have an adverse environmental effect in an area of outstanding scenic attraction.

◄ E

Scalby Against Sewage **SAS**

The SAS supports the European directive to treat waste water before discharging it into the sea. This committee rejects absolutely the Cow Wath Beck site:

- It would be only 400m from housing.
- It would be difficult to guarantee air quality and the avoidance of smells.
- It is next to a public right of way.

The local council eventually chose the Cowlam Hole site. They claimed that 'the preference for a site on the Heritage Coast may appear unusual and contrary to the advice of the Countryside Commission but, weighing up all the key factors on landscape, visibility, design and odour, it is concluded that the Cowlam Hole site is preferable' (*Scarborough Evening News*, 29 November 1997). Work began in September 1998 and has to finish before the EU deadline of 2001.

Activities

1 **a)** Why did Yorkshire Water introduce a waste water disposal scheme in 1991?
   b) How was the new system an improvement on the older system (figure **A**)?
   c) Why were some people in Scarborough displeased with the scheme?

2 Divide your class into two groups: one in favour of the Cow Wath Beck site, the other for Cowlam Hole. Using the information provided, together with the OS map on page 55, each group should prepare a presentation for a class debate about this environmental issue.

3 Your class could adopt a similar approach for a local issue. It could divide into several groups, each representing a different point of view about the issue. Like the SAS action group (figure **D**), each group could organise a campaign producing desktop-published flyers outlining their views, designing posters and conducting questionnaires. Each group could put their case to a mock public meeting held in your classroom.

How can the provision of energy supplies affect the environment?

Coal – an example of a non-renewable energy resource

Non-renewable resources are those, like coal, which can only be used once (*Connections* 56). This means that, at some future time, the resource will run out or, as in South Wales and North-east England, what is left is too expensive to mine.

It was the use of coal as a source of energy that led to the Industrial Revolution, initially in Britain in the early 19th century and later in other coal-producing countries. When coal was first used, little thought was given to the effects it would have on the environment. Then, as now, both the extraction (photo **A**) and the burning (photo **B**) of coal has harmed the environment. Some of these effects are summarised in table **C**.

A

B

C

Extraction of coal	• Opencast mining (photo **A**) creates noise, dust and a scarred landscape.
	• Underground (shaft) mining (*Connections* 20 photo **C**) has unsightly pithead buildings. Waste material is dumped in spoil heaps/tips (south and south-west of Cwm on map **B** page 70) which were unsightly and could be dangerous when wet. (A mudflow at Aberfan in South Wales in 1966 killed 147 people including 116 schoolchildren.)
Use of coal	• Coal is a **fossil** fuel. This means that smoke (soot) and carbon are released when it is burnt.
	• In the 19th century, smoke from industrial/domestic chimneys (*Connections* 40 diagram **A**) blackened buildings and dirtied people's washing.
	• By the late 20th century, it was realised that the release of carbon from power stations and by factories (*Connections* 60–61) caused i) acid rain (which kills trees and fish life and affects buildings – *Connections* 5) and ii) global warming (*Connections* 60–61, *Interactions* 36).
	• Unhealthy for people and wildlife.
	• Waste ash often dumped or allowed to escape into rivers.

Activities

1 a) Why has coal been such an important source of energy?

b) How has i) the extraction and ii) the use of coal affected the environment?

c) Give arguments for and against the continued use of coal as a source of energy.

Wind – an example of a renewable source of energy

Renewable resources are those, like the wind (photo **D**), which are said to be **sustainable** because they can be used over and over again (*Connections* 56–57). Many people in Britain and in other countries feel that we should come to rely much more on these types of energy because:

- being renewable they will never run out
- they cause far less pollution and are much safer than the extraction and burning of fossil fuels and the generation of nuclear power.

However, even the use of wind as a source of energy has its critics. Some of the arguments for and against the development and use of wind power are given in figure **E**.

D

E

In favour

- Wind turbines do not cause air pollution and will reduce the use of fossil fuels.

- Winds are stronger in winter when Britain uses most electricity.

- After the initial cost of building a wind farm, the production of electricity is relatively cheap.

- Wind farms may provide extra income for farmers on whose land they are sited, and may attract jobs to rural areas where there is often a shortage.

- Wind could generate 10 per cent of the UK's total electricity.

Against

- Wind does not blow all the time and electricity generated during storms cannot be stored for use during calm periods.

- Groups of 30-metre-high turbines (wind farms) spoil the scenic attraction of the countryside, especially as they are likely to be located in attractive areas.

- Wind farms are noisy and can interrupt radio and TV reception for people living nearby.

- 7,000 turbines are needed to produce the same amount of electricity as one nuclear power station. 50,000 wind farms may be needed if Britain is to generate 10 per cent of its electricity from this source.

2 Divide your class into four groups. Each group should select one of the following:
- a conservationist worried about the environment
- a farmer on whose land a wind farm is planned
- a tourist wishing to visit an area where several wind farms are planned
- an industrialist in a nearby city who needs a reliable source of cheap electricity.

Each group should, on behalf of the person they represent, consider the possible advantages and disadvantages of wind as a source of energy. A member of each group should be prepared to present their findings to the whole class.

What is the geography of the area around our school?

You can learn and understand a lot of geography by using large-scale maps of the area surrounding your school, and by doing your own local fieldwork. It is impossible, however, in a textbook to provide your local map or to ask questions specific to your local area. Therefore, either use the activities below, based on map **D** opposite, or adapt them to suit your own area.

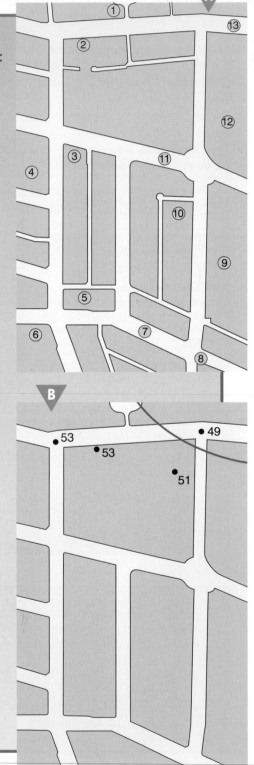

Activities

1. From the letterbox on the corner of Victoria Place and Chatsworth Gardens:
   a) In which direction, as the crow flies, is it to (*Foundations* 92):
      i) the entrance to Trinity School ii) Warwick Road?
   b) How far would you have to walk, in metres, to reach (*Foundations* 94):
      i) the entrance to Trinity School ii) Warwick Road?
   c) Read *Foundations* 106 and then describe the route you would take from Trinity School if you had to post a letter (at L B) and then make a telephone call (at TCB on Warwick Road).
   d) Identify the grid square which contains the most houses and buildings. What is the housing density of this square (refer back to page 61)?

2. Make two larger copies of map **A**.
   a) On the first map, replace the numbers with the correct map symbol, including its colour (*Foundations* 96, 108).
   b) On the second map, again leaving out the numbers, make a key to show the 'Types of land use'. (Only the first five types listed on table **C** column (i) are appropriate to the map opposite, but others, such as industry and shopping, might be found in your local area.)

3. Read *Foundations* 102 and 104, on contours. Make a larger copy of map **B** and then i) add all the remaining spot heights, ii) draw in the 55 m, 60 m, 65 m and 70 m contours (the 50 m contour has already been drawn for you).

4. **Fieldwork** This will involve one, or more, short walks of about 30 minutes around your school. Do take care if you have to cross any roads. You will need *three* larger copies of your local equivalent of map **A**.
   a) On the first map, record the different types of houses. Your key might include those listed in table **C** column (ii).
   b) On the second map, record the building and roofing materials as suggested in table **C** column (iii).
   c) On the third map, record the age of houses. You could divide their ages into those shown in table **C** column (iv). Add the actual date of a house if it is given (usually above the front door).
   d) What changes have been made between the time your OS map was drawn and your fieldwork visit?

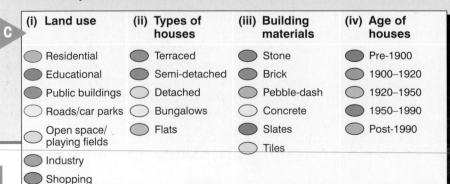

(i) Land use	(ii) Types of houses	(iii) Building materials	(iv) Age of houses
Residential	Terraced	Stone	Pre-1900
Educational	Semi-detached	Brick	1900–1920
Public buildings	Detached	Pebble-dash	1920–1950
Roads/car parks	Bungalows	Concrete	1950–1990
Open space/ playing fields	Flats	Slates	Post-1990
Industry		Tiles	
Shopping			

Each square is 100 metres x 100 metres

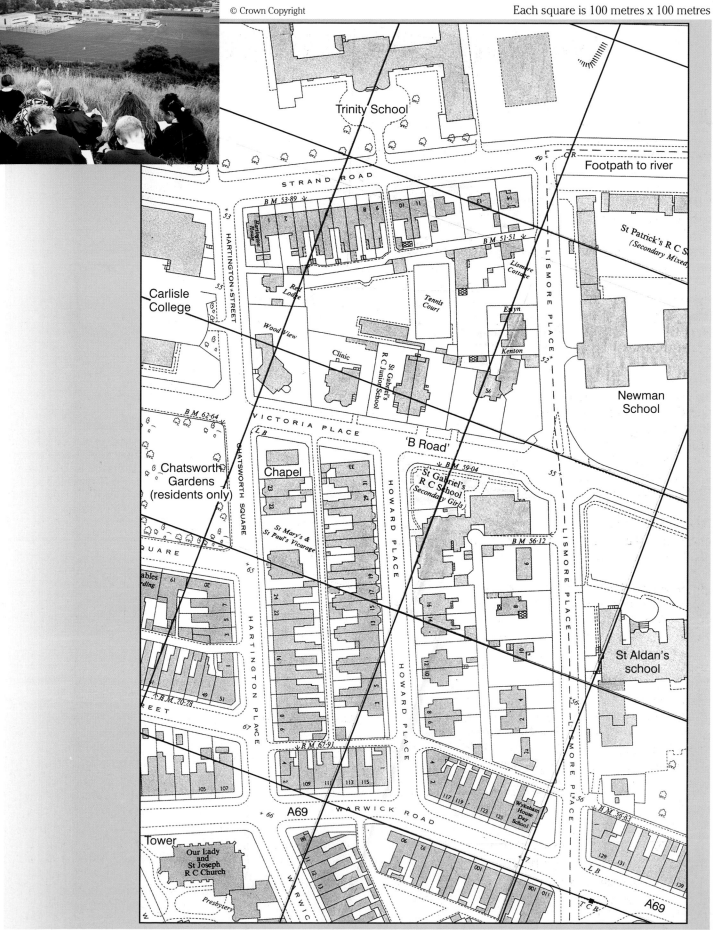

Trinity School

Footpath to river

STRAND ROAD

BM 53·89

Hartington House

Carlisle College

Red Lodge

Wood View

Clinic

Tennis Court

St Gabriel's R C Junior School

BM 51·51

Lismore Cottage

Estyn

Kenton

St Patrick's R C S (Secondary Mixed)

LISMORE PLACE

Newman School

BM 62·64

VICTORIA PLACE

'B Road'

LB

Chatsworth Gardens (residents only)

CHATSWORTH SQUARE

Chapel

St Mary's & St Paul's Vicarage

BM 59·04

St Gabriel's R C School (Secondary Girls)

HOWARD PLACE

BM 56·12

St Aidan's school

SQUARE

ables rding

HARTINGTON PLACE

BM 20·28

BM 67·91

HOWARD PLACE

A69

WARWICK ROAD

Wykeham House Day School

BM 56·63

Tower

Our Lady and St Joseph R C Church

Presbytery

WARWIC

LB

TCB

A69

HARTINGTON STREET

Is there a need for a by-pass?

Enquiry

Does the village of Burniston need a by-pass?
Burniston is a growing village to the north of Scarborough. Locate it on map **A** and on the OS map on page 55. A large and increasing volume of traffic passes through the village along the A171. Pupils at a local school conducted a traffic questionnaire as part of a fieldwork assignment about the village. They found that 48 out of 50 villagers interviewed felt there was too much traffic in Burniston, and that 39 of the 50 felt that the problem could be solved by building a by-pass.

The pupils then conducted a survey which investigated whether or not Burniston needed a by-pass. Groups of pupils counted, for periods of half an hour per group, the type and number of vehicles travelling in either direction along Burniston High Street (photo **B**). They also took photographs of the A171 and recorded their observations about the suitability of the road for the volume and type of traffic using it. The results of one half-hour survey are given in figure **C**. Their findings supported an earlier survey conducted by the Burniston Parish Council in 1975 (figure **D**).

A traffic count was carried out, during August 1975, at a point on the A171 to the north of the junction with the A165 (see OS map). It revealed traffic flows of 10,423 vehicles in a 16-hour period, from 0600 hours to 2200 hours. Approximately 50% of this traffic was by-passable in the sense that its destination was not within the village.

Traffic Survey Record Sheet

Survey site _Burniston High St_   **Date**   **Time** _12–12:30pm_

Type of vehicle	Travelling North (out of Scarborough)	Travelling South (into Scarborough)
Cars	┼┼┼ (110)	┼┼┼ │││ (108)
Vans & Lorries	┼┼┼ ┼┼┼ ┼┼┼ ┼┼┼ ┼┼┼ │││││ (29)	┼┼┼ ┼┼┼ ┼┼┼ ┼┼┼ ┼┼┼ ┼┼┼ ┼┼┼ ┼┼┼ ┼┼┼ ┼┼┼ ┼┼┼ ┼┼┼ ││││ (64)
Buses	│││ (3)	││ (2)
M/cycles	│ (1)	││││ (4)
Tractors	(0)	││ (2)
Totals	143	180

Traffic survey in drive for by-pass

Villagers living near Scarborough are hoping to stage a major traffic count next month in support of a campaign for a by-pass.

There has been concern in many villages, including Scalby, Burniston, Cayton, Ayton, Seamer ..., at the level of traffic and particularly heavy goods vehicles passing through.

Burniston Parish Council has already carried out a survey, with more than 12,000 vehicles on a Sunday and 11,500 on a Tuesday counted in August last year. Chairman Erica Hansom said, 'It is all day, every day during the summer, which makes it quite intolerable.'

Source: *Scarborough Evening News*

Activities

1 Look carefully at the 1:50 000 OS map of Scarborough on page 55, and the atlas map **A** which shows the area around Burniston.
  a) Why do you think so much traffic passes through Burniston?
  b) At what time of year, and for what reason, do you think there is most traffic?

2 Draw a bar graph to show the results of the traffic survey (diagram **C**). If you have access to a computer you could present the results using a spreadsheet and graph.

3 Look carefully at your bar graph, the extract from Burniston council's village plan (figure **D**), the photograph of Burniston High Street (photo **B**) and the article from the *Scarborough Evening News* (figure **E**). Together they should help you answer the following questions.
  a) How much traffic passed through Burniston during the pupils' survey?
  b) Approximately what proportion consisted of larger vehicles such as buses and lorries?

Where should the by-pass go?

A proposal for a Burniston and Cloughton by-pass was first approved by the County Council in 1944, but no final decision has been made. As you saw in *Foundations* 72–73, building a by-pass is expensive, suitable routes have to be planned and meetings with interested groups of people arranged. Figure **F** describes three possible routes that have been suggested for Burniston.

Red Route

This route has been surveyed by the council. Land has been left vacant along the route, ready for development. There would be problems for parts of Burniston, such as that shown in the photograph, as the route crosses part of the village. A flyover would be necessary, damaging the village environment. Large areas of farmland would be isolated from farms.

Blue Route

The use of the existing roads to the west of Burniston and Cloughton would involve the re-alignment and reconstruction of 6.5 km of road. This route would take the by-pass away from the villages and so would have no damaging effect on them. The scale of road-building would have an adverse effect on the character of the rural area. The National Park Officer is concerned about the effect of such a development on the National Park.

© Crown copyright

National Park boundary

Yellow Route

This would involve the construction of 3 km of road along the disused railway line to the east of Burniston and Cloughton. This route would cause less disruption to Burniston. It would, however, separate Cloughton Newlands from the facilities of Cloughton. The disused line is currently used for leisure activities, and is popular with cyclists riding into the National Park. There would be difficulties rejoining the A171 to the north of Cloughton. This route would not serve north-bound traffic on the A171 south of Burniston without a link road joining the A165 and the A171.

A non-by-pass alternative – improvement of the existing A171

The council believe it may be possible to avoid the need for a by-pass by aiding the flow of traffic on the existing A171. This could be achieved by widening some sections of the road, and imposing speed controls and parking restrictions along some lengths. The removal of on-street parking would create problems for local residents. Increased traffic flows would continue to create hazards and cause noise nuisance.

c) Is Burniston High Street suitable for:
i) the volume of traffic ii) the type of traffic?

d) Does the traffic appear to cause any problems for the villagers?

4 a) Look carefully at figure **F**. Explain the possible reactions of the following people to the three proposed by-pass routes:
- a member of the National Park Authority
- the farmer at Low Moor Farm (996931)
- the secretary of the local cycling club
- a Burniston resident living alongside the A171
- a villager living next to the minor road at 007934.

b) Why do you think the Council proposed an alternative to building a by-pass?

c) Divide your class into four groups, each group taking one of the four alternatives shown in figure **F**. Each group needs i) to prepare a presentation in support of their scheme ii) to produce a flyer or poster, possibly using a computer and desktop publishing program, to support their case.
Your class could then debate the issues, ending with a vote as to which alternative they think the local council should choose.

How can you conduct a shopping enquiry in your local CBD?

Enquiry

It was stated in *Foundations* 52 that the centre, or CBD, of a town 'is full of shops, offices, banks and restaurants'. Is this true of your local town or city centre? You will be in a better position to answer that question if you carry out your own enquiry. There are several ways in which you can conduct the enquiry, and many questions that you can ask. The following are meant as suggestions but remember that you should, when conducting any fieldwork, ensure you work in small groups (and not by yourself) and that you are aware of dangers, e.g. traffic.

Examples of hypotheses
1 The CBD is made up of shops and offices.
2 The number of specialist and/or high order shops increases towards the town centre.
3 Certain types of shop are found close to each other, other types are not.
4 The number of pedestrians increases towards the town centre.
5 The closer they live to the town centre, the more frequent and the greater the number of shoppers.
6 The size of shops increases towards the town centre.
7 The town centre is dynamic and is always changing.

How you might conduct your enquiry and record your findings
For most of these activities your class should divide into small groups (photo **A**). Each group will collect data for a small area or from a small number of shoppers. Back at school, this data will be collected together so that as a class you will have covered a much larger area and taken a larger sample.

- **Delimiting the CBD** This can be done by working outwards along roads leading from the CBD. The CBD ends when you come to five consecutive buildings that do not include a shop. Your can draw in the CBD boundary on a 1 : 2500 OS map.
- **Determining the main types of land use and shops** You will need another copy of a 1 : 2500 (or larger) OS map of the city centre. In your given area, plot the ground-floor use of each building. Use the key in diagram **C**. If you have a camera, you could take photos. Back in the classroom you should produce a colour-coded map. It is best to use colours, as this makes the types of land use stand out more clearly, helping you to identify patterns of land use

and types of shop. If you have time, you could produce several coloured maps, each showing a specific land use (e.g. offices) or type of shop (e.g. clothes). You will need to describe and explain any patterns that you find.
- **Number of shoppers** Each group will be given a specific location. It might be in the centre of a street or at a street corner. Record as a tally (as shown on diagram **B**) the number of pedestrians passing you during a 15-minute period (each group must do their recording at the same time). Using the results from each group, draw a flow-line map to show the number of pedestrians. The thickness of the flow lines should be in proportion to the number of pedestrians. Which are the busier streets? Compare these results with your land use survey – is there a correlation (or link) between the two?

A clipboard is really useful when doing fieldwork.

We must remember to be polite when asking people questions.

I'm glad that I came correctly dressed for fieldwork

A

B

CBD LAND USE SURVEY

Type of land use	Code for survey	Colour code
Major shops e.g. department store, M&S, Woolworths, Boots, etc.	A	
Specialist shops e.g. books, sports, jewellers, music, gifts	B	
Clothing & shoe shops	C	
Furniture & carpets	D	
Convenience shops e.g. food, tobacconists, newsagents, sweets	E	
Personal services e.g. hairdresser, shoe repairs, dry cleaner, TV rentals, gas/electricity showrooms, travel agent	F	
Catering & entertainment e.g. cafés, restaurants, hotels, pubs, cinemas	G	
Offices & professional services e.g. banks, solicitors, estate agents, opticians, doctors	H	
Public buildings & offices e.g. library, Town Hall, Post Office, Police Station, Job Centre, info. office	I	
Transport e.g. car parks, bus/rail station	J	
Change e.g. vacant premises, derelict, under construction	K	

Location:
Date:

	Shopper		
	1	2	3
1. Where have you come from? name of town, village, or district			
2. How did you travel to the centre? a-bus, b-car, c-taxi, d-walk, e-other			
3. How frequently do you shop here? a-daily, b-2/3 times a week, c-weekly, d-2/3 times a month, e-monthly, f-less often			
4. What are you shopping for? a-clothes/footwear, b-electrical goods, c-food, d-general, e-gifts, f-services, g-other			
5. Which supermarket do you use? a-Safeway, b-Tesco, c-Morrisons, d-Kwik-save,e-Sainsburys, f-other			
6. How frequently do you go there? a-daily, b-2/3 times a week, c-weekly, d-2/3 times a month, e-monthly, f-less often			
7. Which other shopping centre do you use? name of city, or centre			
8. How frequently do you go there? a-daily, b-2/3 times a week, c-weekly, d-2/3 times a month, e-monthly, f-less often			
Rate each of the following aspects of this centre on a 6-point scale 1-very poor, 2-poor, 3-quite good, 4-good, 5-very good, 6-excellent			
9. Overall variety of shops			
10. Range of clothes/shoe shops			
11. Access to public transport			
12. Car parking			
13. General appearance of centre			
14. What improvements would you like to see to the centre ?			

- **Shop size** As a class, decide *either* to count the number of storeys *or* to pace out the shop frontage for each shop in the street where you did your pedestrian count. Plot your class findings on a graph.

- **Types of shopper** Use a questionnaire similar to that in diagram **D** (if you get the total class sample to come to 50 or 100 then it is easier to work out percentages). All your class can enter their results onto a prepared computer database, and then use it to create a spreadsheet to chart some of the questionnaire results. Draw pie charts, or other suitable graphs, to show your results. You could word-process a description of your results (as was suggested for the 'weather' enquiry on page 33).

- **Recent changes** What changes can you, or your class, remember having taken place recently in the CBD? List the changes under headings like land use (e.g. a shop becoming an office), shop type (e.g. shoe shop becoming an optician's), traffic access (e.g. new one-way system) or improvements to the environment (e.g. addition of seats and flowerbeds).

- **Future improvements** This is an opportunity to be a town planner, by using the data from your questionnaire. You could also obtain other people's opinions from the letter page of your local newspaper.

- **Conclusions** These should show, together with reasons, whether the data you collected agreed or disagreed with your original hypotheses.

Why is drawing fieldsketches an important geographical skill?

In *Foundations* 10–11 you were introduced to a variety of ways by which you could describe a place, one of which was to draw a labelled **fieldsketch**. Fieldsketching is an important technique which can be used, when conducting fieldwork, for the recording and presentation of data. It encourages you, after carefully observing a landscape, to select and record important geographical features. Fieldsketches are best drawn from a vantage, or **viewpoint**, e.g. the top of a hill or a tall building. Many of you, when asked to draw a fieldsketch, plead 'but I can't draw'. This is rarely true – most of us are far better than we think. To help you improve your technique, follow the stages in figure **A**. Begin by finding a suitable vantage-point. You can do this by using a 1:50 000 OS map, especially if it includes the symbol for a viewpoint (diagram **B**). The photo in figure **A** was taken from the side of Scarborough Castle (049891 on page 55) with the camera facing south-west. Find the grid reference point and compare the photo with the map.

A

B

1 Find a vantage point. Begin by looking carefully at the view, and pick out key features with the use of an OS map.

2
a Draw the horizon line $\frac{2}{3}$ up the page.
b Look carefully at the view and decide on the limits of your sketch.
c Draw the key features to provide a framework for your sketch.

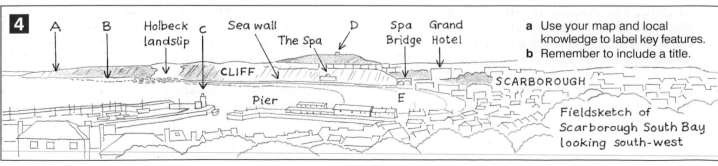

3 Add more detail to your sketch, drawing in key features.

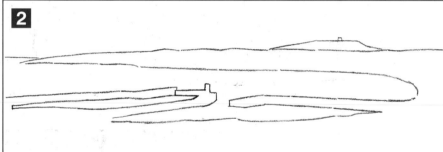

4
a Use your map and local knowledge to label key features.
b Remember to include a title.

Fieldsketch of Scarborough South Bay looking south-west

When you have completed the first four stages in the field you should, either back at school or at home, redraw the fieldsketch neatly, adding labels where appropriate and using sensible colours to identify and highlight key features (Activity 1). Diagram **C** is an excellent example of a well-drawn and accurately labelled fieldsketch.

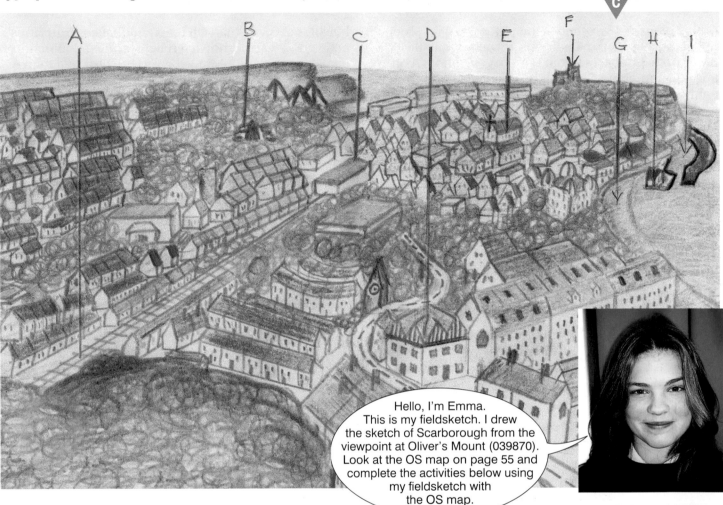

Hello, I'm Emma. This is my fieldsketch. I drew the sketch of Scarborough from the viewpoint at Oliver's Mount (039870). Look at the OS map on page 55 and complete the activities below using my fieldsketch with the OS map.

Activities

1 Look again at the photo and the final fieldsketch in diagram **A**, together with the OS map of the area on page 55. Identify, name and give the six-figure grid reference for each of the following:
- the headland at A
- the coastal feature at B
- the human feature at C
- the hill with a viewpoint at D
- the bay at E.

2 Emma's fieldsketch (diagram **C**) was taken from the viewpoint at Oliver's Mount. Locate Oliver's Mount on the 1:50 000 OS map on page 55.
   a) What is the six-figure reference of Oliver's Mount?
   b) In which direction was Emma facing when she drew her fieldsketch?
   c) Using the OS map and the fieldsketch together, identify the features which Emma has labelled A to I.

3 a) Look at photo **A** on page 54. It is an example of an **oblique aerial photograph**, as it is taken from a plane and looking down on Scarborough at an angle. Using this photo (or any other of the numerous oblique photos used in the Key Geography series), draw a carefully labelled fieldsketch.
   b) Draw a fieldsketch in your local area. It could be of, or from, your school; within the place, or the surrounding area, where you live; or it could be a specific human or physical feature. Make sure that your vantage-point is safe. It is best, if possible, to visit the fieldsketch location on a clear day, remembering to take with you a sketch pad, pen and pencil and an OS map to help you identify the key features that you wish to label. If the weather is wet, you may be able to buy a local postcard; if it is fine you might take a photo in case you need to remind yourself of the view.

How can you conduct a river or coastal enquiry?

Connections 8–13 describes the processes that produce river landscapes and landforms. If you refer, in this order in that book, to photo **B** on page 8, photo **A** on page 96 and photo **E** on page 13, you will notice how the height and steepness of the valley sides, and the width of the valley floor, change from source to mouth. These changes in height and steepness can also be seen on a map. *Foundations* 102–105 explains how

height is shown on an OS map and that **contour lines** are a good way of showing relief features. Contour lines can also help you to draw a **cross-section** (diagram **A**). A cross-section is a view of the landscape as it would appear if it were sliced open (see Stage 4 in diagram **A**), or the shape of the land if you were to walk over it.

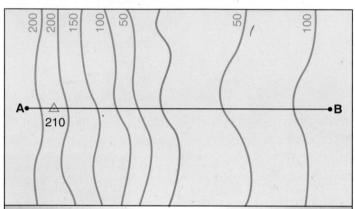

Stage 1
Locate the section line A–B on the map. Look carefully at the contours to find the highest and lowest points (needed for your vertical scale) and to see if, and where, the land is rising or falling.

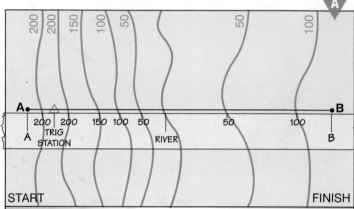

Stage 2
Place the straight edge of a piece of paper between the two end-points of the section. Carefully mark the point where each contour crosses the paper. Label the contour heights on the paper (on steeper slopes you may only be able to label alternate contours). Mark on other important features, e.g. rivers.

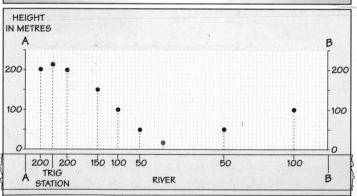

Stage 3
Place the straight edge of the paper against a horizontal line of equal length drawn, preferably, on graph paper. Use as a vertical scale on the graph paper either 1 cm = 100 metres for a 1:50 000 map, or 1 cm = 50 metres for a 1:25 000 map (otherwise your section will look like the Himalayas!). Mark on the graph paper, using small dots (or crosses), the height of the contours (and any other feature).

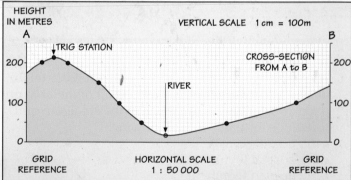

Stage 4
Join the dots together with a smooth, freehand curve (do *not* use a ruler). Notice the smooth curve for hilltops and valley floors. Use arrows to help label any features. Add six-figure grid references for the two end-points. Remember to add a title and the horizontal and vertical scales.

Cross-sections, drawn at different parts of a valley, can show how a valley changes its shape. Referring to the OS map on page 55, find the viewpoint at the northern end of the Forge Valley (983876). At this point the valley has

steep sides and, as shown on fieldsketch **E** on page 107, a V shape. If you follow the valley southwards to the villages of East and West Ayton, you can see how the valley widens and the sides get less steep and less high.

Enquiry

Further evidence about how river processes and landforms change can be collected from fieldwork. Diagram **B** shows groups of pupils conducting a range of experiments. Each member of each group should know exactly what they have to do and each group should have one member recording the results. The groups are supervised and supported by members of staff, and the whole party have considered health and safety procedures. Everyone is dressed correctly with warm and waterproof clothing. Pupils in the river are wearing waders and are being watched at all times.

B

Group A is finding the cross-section of the channel. Two pupils are measuring the river's width with a tape. A third is measuring the depth at 0.5 metre intervals.

Group B is measuring channel gradient. They marked a standard distance along the bank, and are working out the angle with a theodolite or clinometer and a sighting pole.

Group C is measuring the speed (velocity) of the river. They marked a measured distance on the bank, and now, with stopwatches, are timing how long it takes an orange to travel between the two points.

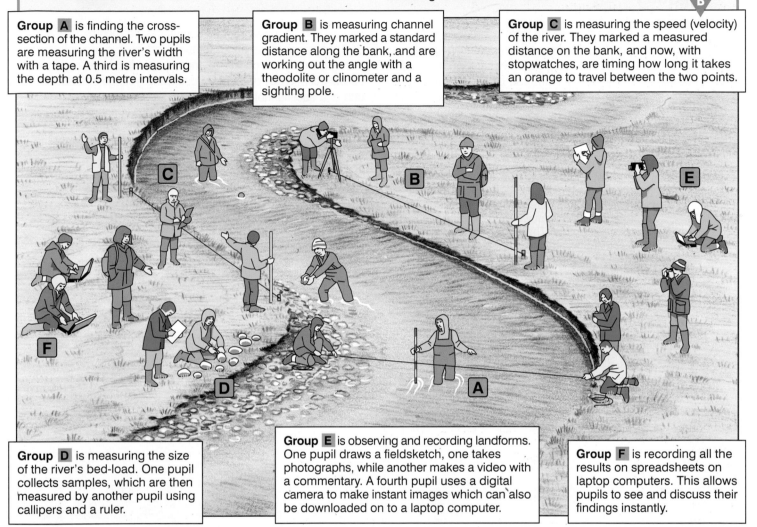

Group D is measuring the size of the river's bed-load. One pupil collects samples, which are then measured by another pupil using callipers and a ruler.

Group E is observing and recording landforms. One pupil draws a fieldsketch, one takes photographs, while another makes a video with a commentary. A fourth pupil uses a digital camera to make instant images which can also be downloaded on to a laptop computer.

Group F is recording all the results on spreadsheets on laptop computers. This allows pupils to see and discuss their findings instantly.

Activities

1 Re-read *Connections* 8–13 and then suggest key questions, or hypotheses, that the pupils could be investigating in diagram **B**.

2 You may be able to conduct similar fieldwork activities, and to use some of the techniques described in diagram **B**, in your local area.
   a) Remember, before you begin, to be sure you know exactly what you want to achieve, that you have the correct equipment and clothing, and that you are aware of the dangers of working in and near rivers.
   b) Ideally you should conduct your experiments in at least two different parts of the river's course in order to see possible changes.

3 Are you a geographer yet? If you are, you should have developed an enquiring mind and be able to ask yourself, and other people, geographical questions. *Connections* 14–15 explains the formation of coastal landscapes, with photo **A** showing the landscape at Old Harry's Rocks, in Dorset.
   a) What key questions, or hypotheses, might you be able to investigate while on a field visit to this area, or to your local coast?
   b) What surveys could you conduct to test these key questions?

4 Using the OS map on page 55, draw two cross-sections of different parts of the Forge Valley.

How can you conduct a local farm enquiry?

Enquiry

In *Connections* you investigated the factors that influence different types of farming and how farming can change the landscape. You can extend those enquiries through a field visit to a specific farm. Thorn Park Farm, run by Mr Wilson, is a dairy farm to the west of Scarborough (map reference 984882 on the OS map, page 55). Its boundaries, formed by the Sea Cut, two minor roads and a footpath, are shown on map **C** and can be located on the OS map. Pupils from one local school spent a day at the farm collecting a range of data. As part of a questionnaire, pupils asked Mr Wilson why he concentrated on dairying. His reply is given in figure **A**.

'The climate is well suited to good grass growth, with a balance of sunshine and rainfall. The farm is near the coast, so in winter we have less frost and in summer there are plenty of showers. The surrounding hills provide shelter from winds. The valley floor is relatively flat and easier to manage. The soils here are variable and therefore, along with the weather, cannot always support arable crops. The farm is accessible by road, so it is relatively easy for a milk tanker to collect the milk and take it to the dairy for processing. My father and I have always been dairy farmers.'

A

B

Thorn Park Farm Land Use Code

1. GRASSLAND				
Grass cut for silage	mk on map	**Gl**	colour	Green
Grass for grazing	mk on map	**GP**	colour	Orange
2. ARABLE LAND				
Cereals (wheat, barley, oats)	mk on map	**A**	colour	Yellow
Green fodder (e.g. kale)	mk on map	**Aka**	colour	Grey
3. MARKET GARDENING				
Allotments & soft fruits	mk on map	**M**	colour	Purple
4. HEATHLAND, MOORLAND, ROUGH LAND				
....	mk on map	**H**	colour	Brown
5. WOODLAND				
....	mk on map	**W**	colour	DK green
6. WATER & MARSH				
....	mk on map	**WM**	colour	Blue

The pupils conducted a land use survey of the farm, plotting, with the aid of a code (figure **B**), the use made of each field. Back at school, the pupils were able to produce a colour-coded map which enabled them to identify any possible land use patterns (map **C**).

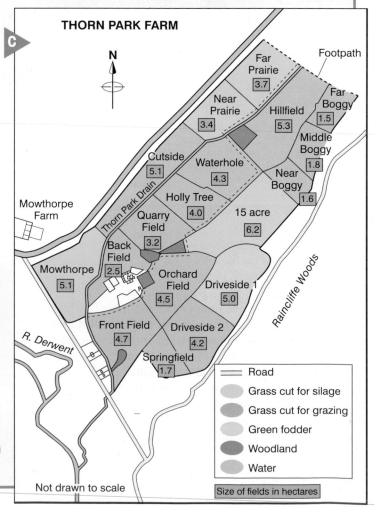

C

THORN PARK FARM

N

Footpath

Far Prairie 3.7
Near Prairie 3.4
Hillfield 5.3
Far Boggy 1.5
Middle Boggy 1.8
Near Boggy 1.6
Cutside 5.1
Waterhole 4.3
Holly Tree 4.0
15 acre 6.2
Mowthorpe Farm
Thorn Park Drain
Quarry Field 3.2
Back Field 2.5
Mowthorpe 5.1
Orchard Field 4.5
Driveside 1 5.0
Raincliffe Woods
Front Field 4.7
Driveside 2 4.2
R. Derwent
Springfield 1.7

Road
Grass cut for silage
Grass cut for grazing
Green fodder
Woodland
Water

Not drawn to scale

Size of fields in hectares

Pupils also conducted a farm building survey, observing and recording on a sketch plan the use made of each building, and taking photographs. Mr Wilson demonstrated how he milked the cows (photo **D**). This job, the most important on the farm, is done twice a day at 0600 and 1700 hours every day of the year. It takes about one and a half hours to milk the 90 or so cows. The pupils asked Mr Wilson what he was trying to achieve on the farm. They were surprised by his answer. Due to the fall in prices for cows and calves as a result of the BSE scare, and a drop of 20 per cent in subsidies which he receives for milk, Mr Wilson's short-term aim was 'just to survive'.

Activities

1 a) Using the OS map on page 55, draw a large labelled sketch map to show the site and situation of Thorn Park Farm. Include on your sketch the site of the farm, the surrounding hills, the minor roads bordering the farm, the Sea Cut, the National Park boundary, Forge Valley, the built-up area of Scarborough, and the coast.

b) In figure **A**, Mr Wilson explained why he thinks the area is suited to dairying. Add, as labels, any suitable points to your sketch map.

2 a) Using the OS map, draw a cross-section (page 104) across the farm from Suffield Ings (983893) to the footpath at Skell Dikes (987873). Label, on your section, two areas of woodland, any high land, the Sea Cut, the rise on which the farm buildings are sited, two steep slopes, and a minor road.

b) Diagram **E** is Simon's fieldsketch of the farm. Re-draw his sketch replacing the letters with the appropriate features from the following list:
● Raincliffe Woods ● Forge Valley
● pasture land ● the river ● the farmhouse
● the barn ● a minor road.

3 a) Using information on this page and pages 68–69, together with your sketch map, fieldsketch and cross-section, explain why Thorn Park is a dairy farm.

b) Which of the physical and human factors outlined in *Connections* 24–25, do you consider to be the most important to Mr Wilson at Thorn Park Farm?

4 a) Look at map **C** which gives the area of each field. Calculate the percentage of each type of land use, giving your answer in the form of a pie graph.

b) Describe and explain the main types of land use on the farm. How do you account for the names given to various fields?

5 a) Why is Mr Wilson merely 'trying to survive'? Try to find out about changes that are affecting farming at the present time.

b) *Either*
i) Your class may be able to visit a farm in your local area, in which case you could conduct investigations similar to those done at Thorn Park Farm *or*
ii) If you have access to the Internet, the National Farmers Union has an excellent education web site at:

http://www.nfu.org.uk/

It usually has information about various farms, giving, for example, a profile of the farm, an OS map and a land use map, and a collection of aerial photographs.

Hello, I'm Simon. This is my fieldsketch. I drew the sketch to show the site and situation of Thorn Park Farm as part of my Year 8 fieldwork. Compare my sketch with the OS map on page 55. I drew my fieldsketch near the footpath along the Sea Cut at grid reference 982883. I was looking south-east.

11 New Zealand, an economically developed country

What are the main physical features of New Zealand?

The most lasting image of New Zealand is its scenery. The scenery includes mountains, glaciers and fiords in South Island; volcanoes in North Island; and rivers, lakes and a spectacular coastline across the whole country (map A).

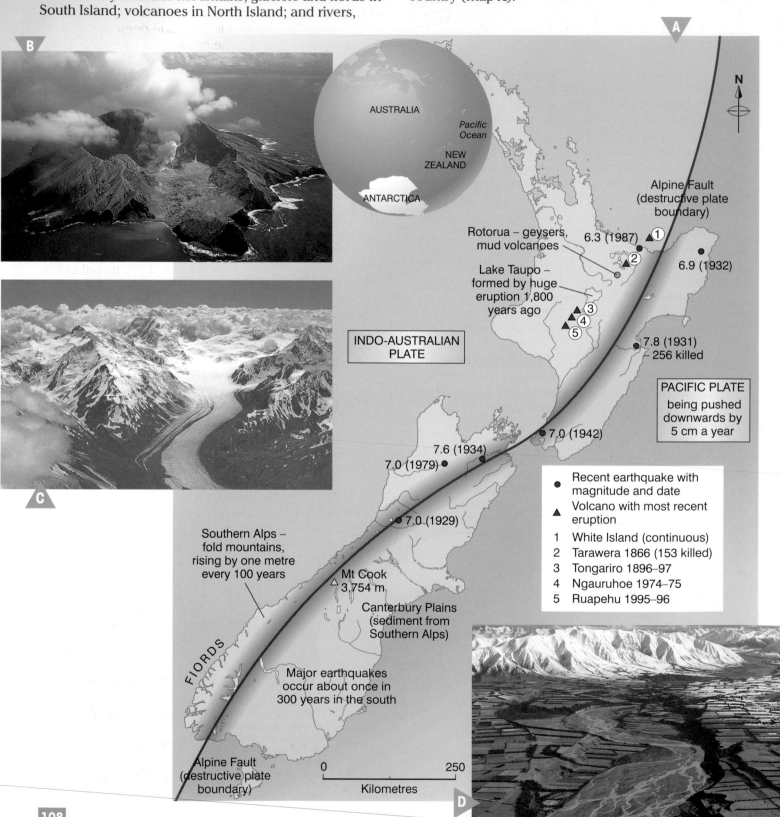

AUSTRALIA

Pacific Ocean

NEW ZEALAND

ANTARCTICA

N

Alpine Fault (destructive plate boundary)

Rotorua – geysers, mud volcanoes

6.3 (1987)

6.9 (1932)

Lake Taupo – formed by huge eruption 1,800 years ago

3

4

5

7.8 (1931) – 256 killed

INDO-AUSTRALIAN PLATE

PACIFIC PLATE being pushed downwards by 5 cm a year

7.0 (1942)

7.6 (1934)

7.0 (1979)

7.0 (1929)

Southern Alps – fold mountains, rising by one metre every 100 years

Mt Cook △ 3,754 m

Canterbury Plains (sediment from Southern Alps)

FIORDS

Major earthquakes occur about once in 300 years in the south

Alpine Fault (destructive plate boundary)

● Recent earthquake with magnitude and date

▲ Volcano with most recent eruption

1 White Island (continuous)
2 Tarawera 1866 (153 killed)
3 Tongariro 1896–97
4 Ngauruhoe 1974–75
5 Ruapehu 1995–96

0   250
Kilometres

New Zealand is located at the boundary of the Indo-Australian and Pacific Plates (map **E** page 5).

- In North Island the two plates meet at a destructive plate margin (diagram **E** page 7). The Pacific Plate, moving westwards by some 5 cm a year, is forced downwards under the Indo-Australian Plate. In doing so it causes earthquakes and forms volcanoes. On average an earthquake with a magnitude greater than 6.0 (diagram **B** page 6) occurs once a year, and one of 7.0 or over every ten years. The volcanoes form part of the Pacific 'Ring of Fire' (*Connections* 26) and include five between White Island (photo **B**) and Ruapehu (diagram **C** page 11) which have erupted in the last 100 years or so. The Rotorua region is noted for its geysers and mud volcanoes (photo **E**).

- In South Island the convergence of the two plates has pushed the crust upwards to form the fold mountains of the Southern Alps (photo **D**). At present the mountains are rising by 1 metre in 100 years, and the east coast is moving towards the west by 1 metre in 40 years.

South Island has been heavily glaciated. There are still over 300 glaciers (the longest, the Tasman glacier, is 30 km in length), numerous large and deep glacial lakes and, indented into the south-west coast, fiords (page 112). Material from the mountains has been deposited in the east by glaciers and rivers to form the flat Canterbury Plains (photo **D** and page 114).

Apart from the extreme north, which is subtropical, much of New Zealand has a temperate climate. Surrounded by the sea and with the prevailing winds from the west (pages 28–29), the climate is not unlike that of the UK (map **A** page 34). Except in the mountains, temperatures are rarely extreme and sunshine totals are often high (map **F**). Rain, mainly relief and frontal (page 31), falls fairly evenly throughout the year. Amounts, especially in South Island, are greater on the west coast than the east (map **G**). Snowfall can be heavy in mountainous areas during winter and can lie all year at altitude.

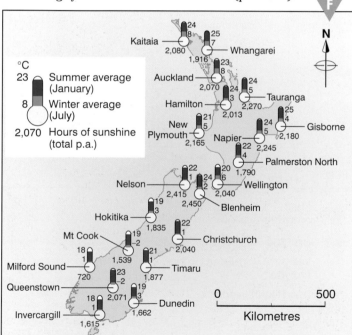

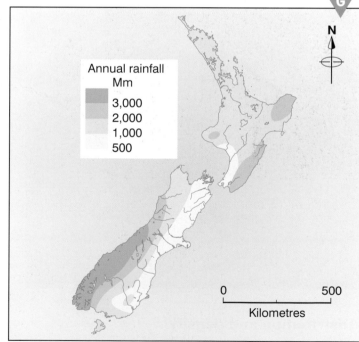

Activities

1 Explain, with the help of a labelled diagram, why:
   a) earthquakes and
   b) volcanoes
   occur in New Zealand.

2 a) Why are temperatures mild throughout the year in New Zealand?
   b) Why do most parts of New Zealand get rain throughout the year?
   c) Why does: i) the west coast of New Zealand get more rainfall than the east
      ii) the Southern Alps receive heavy snowfall?

What are the main human features of New Zealand?

The movement of people into New Zealand

- The first Polynesian migration into New Zealand occurred over 1,000 years ago when Maori people began arriving by canoe after epic journeys across parts of the Pacific Ocean (map **A** and photo **B**).
- The next major immigration, which began in the early nineteenth century, saw the arrival of Europeans, most of whom were British.
- A second wave of Polynesian migration came after the Second World War when Pacific Islanders, many from Western Samoa, were encouraged to come to work in New Zealand. (In 1996, 82 per cent of Niueans lived in New Zealand and only 18 per cent in Niue itself. The comparable figures for Cook Islanders was 64 and 36 per cent.)
- Since 1990 there has been a sharp increase in immigrants from South-east Asia. In 1995, more Taiwanese were granted New Zealand residency than were British.

Graph **C** shows New Zealand's ethnic make-up at the 1996 census.

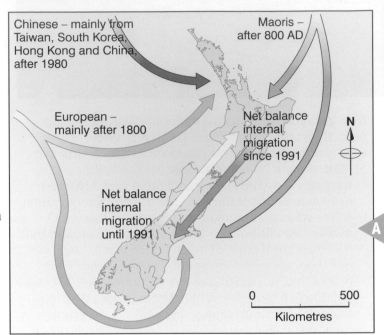

Chinese – mainly from Taiwan, South Korea, Hong Kong and China, after 1980

Maoris – after 800 AD

European – mainly after 1800

Net balance internal migration since 1991

Net balance internal migration until 1991

N

0   500
Kilometres

A

B

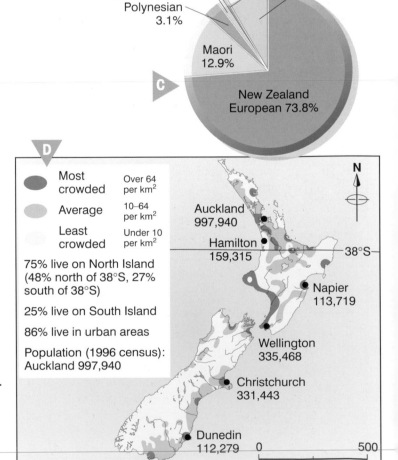

Chinese 1.1%   Indian 0.8%

Others 8.3%

Pacific Island Polynesian 3.1%

Maori 12.9%

C

New Zealand European 73.8%

Distribution and density

We have already seen (page 43) that the world's population is not spread out evenly. In comparison with other countries, New Zealand has a relatively low population density, with only 14 people living on each square kilometre (compared with the UK's 241 per km²). Most of the country's population is concentrated in the north of North Island (map **D**), with one in seven inhabitants living in the Auckland region. Many parts of South Island are sparsely populated.

D

Most crowded	Over 64 per km²	
Average	10–64 per km²	
Least crowded	Under 10 per km²	

75% live on North Island (48% north of 38°S, 27% south of 38°S)

25% live on South Island

86% live in urban areas

Population (1996 census): Auckland 997,940

Auckland 997,940
Hamilton 159,315
38°S
Napier 113,719
Wellington 335,468
Christchurch 331,443
Dunedin 112,279

N

0   500
Kilometres

How is New Zealand's population changing?

Figure **E** shows that New Zealand's population has grown at a slow, but fairly steady, rate during the twentieth century. This is partly because, like other economically developed countries, it has a low birth rate, a low death rate and, therefore, a low natural increase in population (page 44). It is also because, during this period, New Zealand has only had a small net gain in migrants (page 52). Indeed since 1980 there has been a reversal with, for the first time, more emigrants than immigrants.

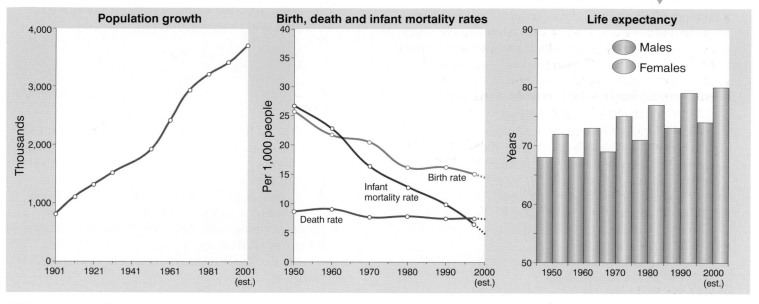

What is New Zealand's population structure?

New Zealand's population structure (graph **F**) shows that:

- about one-quarter of the total population is aged under 15 – this is higher than most developed countries, and is expected to decrease during the next few decades
- one in eight of the total population is aged 65 and over – it is predicted that the total number in this age group will rise from its present 416,000 (12 per cent) to 940,000 by the year 2031 (19 per cent).

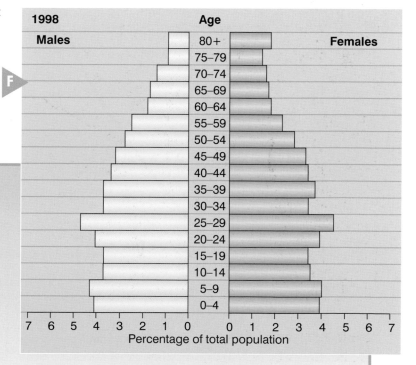

Activities

1 **a)** Which were the first group of people to settle in New Zealand?
   b) What proportion of the country's population do they represent today?
   c) Why do people of European origins form the largest ethnic group?
   d) From which country have most immigrants arrived since 1995?

2 Try to find out why:
   a) nearly half of New Zealand's population live in the north of North Island (think about relief, climate, resources, transport, services and interdependence with other countries)
   b) many parts of South Island are sparsely populated (think of the clues offered in part **a)** and see pages 112–113).

3 With the help of figure **E** above and page 45, describe how the shape of New Zealand's population pyramid (graph **F**) shows that the country has: i) a low birth rate ii) a low infant mortality rate iii) a low natural increase iv) a long life expectancy.

What are the physical characteristics of two regions in New Zealand?

Physical similarities and differences

It is difficult to select only two contrasting regions in New Zealand. For example, North Island has its volcanic area which contrasts with its subtropical beaches and islands, while South Island has its mountains, fiords and glaciers which likewise contrast with an extensive flat plain (maps **A** and cross-sections **B**).

Geomorphological processes and landforms

Western South Island

- Fold mountains formed at the boundary of the Pacific and Indo-Australian Plates (map **A** page 108).
- Glaciers, which form rugged peaks and carve out deep valleys (photo **C** and, on page 108, photo **C**).
- Steep coastal cliffs and, in the south-west, fiords (photo **E** and, on page 84, figure **A**). Fiords are glaciated valleys which have been drowned by a rise in sea-level.
- Rivers are short and many plunge as waterfalls into the sea (figure **A** page 84).

Eastern South Island

- Foothills of the mountains and, in the east, a flat plain formed by material brought down from the mountains (photo **D** and, on page 108, photo **D**).
- A more gentle coastline (photo **F**) with, in the north, rias. Rias are river valleys that have been drowned by a rise in sea-level.
- Rivers are long and, following snowmelt, carry a lot of material which is later deposited (when levels fall), creating numerous channels (photo **D** page 108).

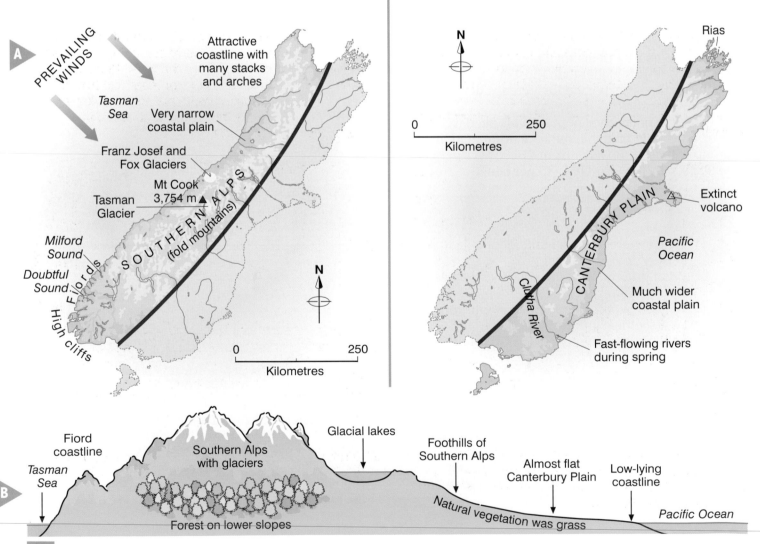

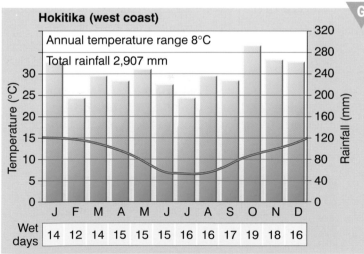

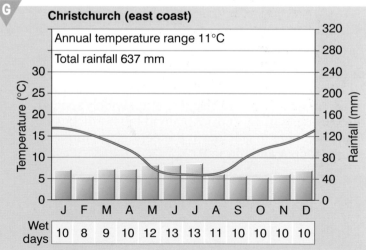

Climate

West coast

The graphs **G** for Hokitika on the west coast and Christchurch on the east coast show that temperatures are mild in winter and relatively warm in summer. The low annual range in temperature reflects the moderating influence of the sea (page 28). Temperatures are much lower in the mountains where it may be cold enough for snow to lie throughout the year.

East coast

However, the west coast is much wetter than the east. This is due to the combination of prevailing winds and depressions which come from the west. Places like Hokitika receive large amounts of relief and frontal rain (snow in the mountains), while places to the east of the mountains receive much less as they are in a rainshadow area (page 31).

G

Hokitika (west coast)

Annual temperature range 8°C

Total rainfall 2,907 mm

Wet days	14	12	14	15	15	15	16	16	17	19	18	16
	J	F	M	A	M	J	J	A	S	O	N	D

Christchurch (east coast)

Annual temperature range 11°C

Total rainfall 637 mm

Wet days	10	8	9	10	12	13	13	11	10	10	10	10
	J	F	M	A	M	J	J	A	S	O	N	D

Activities

1 What are i) the similarities and ii) the differences in: **a)** geomorphological processes and **b)** landforms between the west of South Island and the east?

2 What are **a)** the similarities and **b)** the differences in climate between the west of South Island and the east?

What are the human characteristics of two regions in New Zealand?

Human and economic similarities and differences

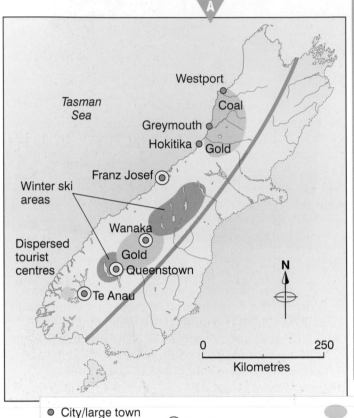

Population

Differences in population density between the west and east of South Island are shown on map **D** on page 110.

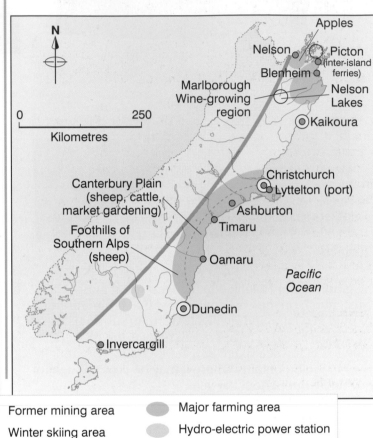

● City/large town	Former mining area	Major farming area
○ Tourist resort/centre		
● Small town	Winter skiing area	Hydro-electric power station

Settlement

West coast

A few small towns and villages, often widely spaced out. A long, narrow coastal plain to the north, beside lakes and near to glaciers in the centre and further south (map **A** and photo **B**).

East coast

Several cities and large towns along the coast. Numerous smaller settlements often located inland. Individual sheep stations and wine-producing estates (map **A** and photo **C**).

Economic activities

West coast

Primary – formerly i) gold near Arrowtown (photo **B**), Hokitika and Greymouth and ii) coal at Greymouth. Very little farming or commercial forestry.

Secondary – jade ornaments, otherwise relatively limited.

Tertiary – important for tourism. Tourists are attracted to glaciers (e.g. Franz Josef, photo **C** page 113), fiords (e.g. Milford Sound, photo **E** page 113), and restored mining towns (e.g. Arrowtown, photo **B**). Queenstown (photo **D**) is a major tourist centre for long-distance trekking, jet-boating, skiing (winter) and bungy jumping.

East coast

Primary – important farming areas include i) the Marlborough region noted for its white wine (photo **E**), ii) Canterbury Plain with its intensive sheep, cattle and market gardening (photo **D** page 113), iii) the foothills of the Southern Alps with their large sheep stations (photo **F**) and iv) Nelson, which is important for apples.

Secondary – mainly the processing of agricultural produce (wine, butter).

Tertiary – employs many people living in the larger towns and cities, e.g. in commerce, health, education and transport.

Environment

Exactly half of New Zealand's 38 National Parks and two World Heritage Areas are in South Island (map **G**).

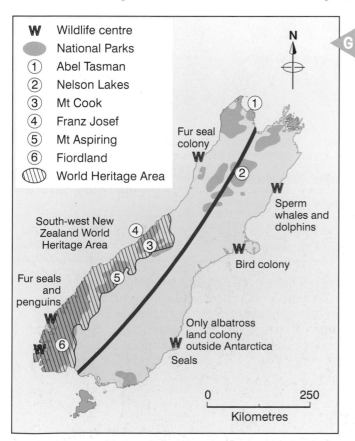

W   Wildlife centre
National Parks
① Abel Tasman
② Nelson Lakes
③ Mt Cook
④ Franz Josef
⑤ Mt Aspiring
⑥ Fiordland
World Heritage Area

Fur seal colony
Sperm whales and dolphins
South-west New Zealand World Heritage Area
Bird colony
Fur seals and penguins
Only albatross land colony outside Antarctica
Seals

0   250
Kilometres

Activities

1 What are i) the similarities and ii) the differences in:
   a) population distribution
   b) settlement and
   c) economic activities between the west of South Island and the east?

2 a) How can you explain the large number of National Parks in South Island?
   b) What do you think are the reasons why the South Island was designated a World Heritage Area?

How developed and how interdependent is New Zealand?

How developed is New Zealand?

By now you should be aware that the term **development** is not an easy one to define. To many people it means how rich a country is and how high the standard of living is for its people. The wealth of a country is given by the **gross national product (GNP)** per person, expressed in US dollars (page 76, *Interactions* 86, *Places* 7). As shown in figure **A**, New Zealand is one of the world's richer countries and is, therefore, in terms of wealth, considered to be economically developed.

However, wealth is not the only way that development may be measured. It can also be measured, and described, by differences in employment (*Interactions* 86–87), trade, population, health and education (*Places* 8–11, 61 and 109). Yet each of these measures can in turn be linked to the wealth of a country as the richer it is, the more money it will have to spend on such things as schools, hospitals and imports (diagram **B**).

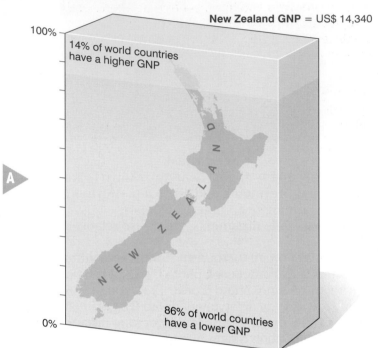

New Zealand GNP = US$ 14,340

100%

14% of world countries have a higher GNP

A

86% of world countries have a lower GNP

0%

B

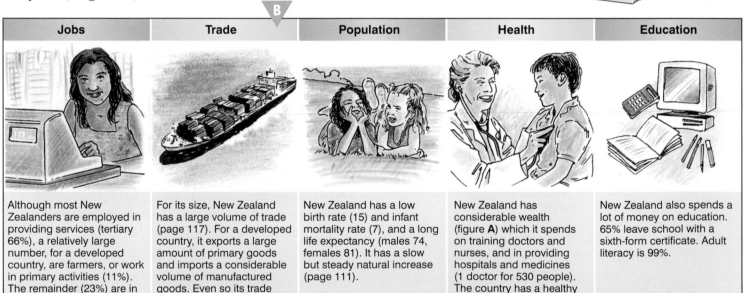

Jobs	Trade	Population	Health	Education
Although most New Zealanders are employed in providing services (tertiary 66%), a relatively large number, for a developed country, are farmers, or work in primary activities (11%). The remainder (23%) are in the secondary sector (page 66).	For its size, New Zealand has a large volume of trade (page 117). For a developed country, it exports a large amount of primary goods and imports a considerable volume of manufactured goods. Even so its trade balance is almost even (diagram **C**).	New Zealand has a low birth rate (15) and infant mortality rate (7), and a long life expectancy (males 74, females 81). It has a slow but steady natural increase (page 111).	New Zealand has considerable wealth (figure **A**) which it spends on training doctors and nurses, and in providing hospitals and medicines (1 doctor for 530 people). The country has a healthy diet and people live an active life.	New Zealand also spends a lot of money on education. 65% leave school with a sixth-form certificate. Adult literacy is 99%.

How interdependent is New Zealand?

As was explained on page 82, no country is likely to have everything that it needs to make it totally independent. Instead, countries have to become **interdependent**. This is when they either work together or have to rely upon others if they wish to improve their standard of living and quality of life. One way by which countries become interdependent is through trade (page 82, *Interactions* 88, *Places* 58 and 106).

Mainly because of its isolated geographical position, New Zealand's economy is heavily dependent upon trade. In recent years, New Zealand has had a **trade surplus** – that is, it has earned sufficient money from its exports to enable it to pay for its imports (figure **C**).

Although New Zealand's trade surplus is an indicator of a developed country, the actual types of goods that it exports and imports (diagram **D**) are more typical of a developing country (diagram **A** page 82). Remember that a developing country is more likely to export primary products and import manufactured goods (Kenya, *Places* 58) whereas a developed country usually exports manufactured goods and imports primary products (Japan, *Places* 106).

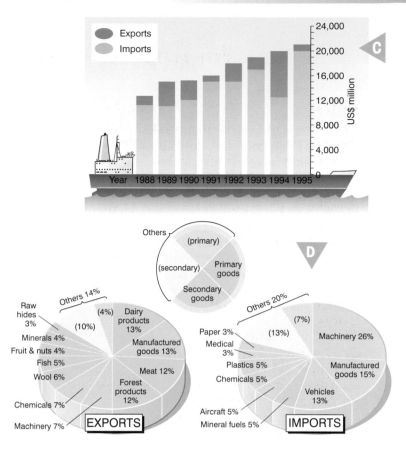

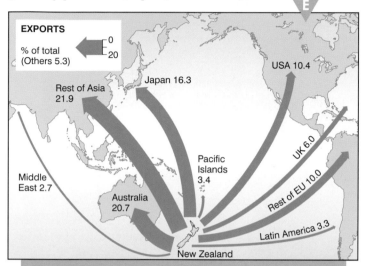

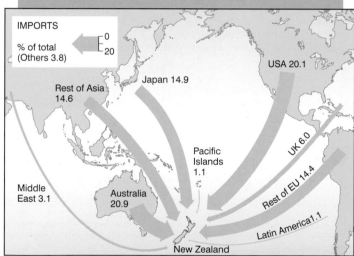

During the 1960s (before Britain joined the European Community), 51 per cent of New Zealand's exports went to the UK, and 40 per cent of its imports came from there. Traditionally meat (Canterbury lamb), wool and dairy produce (butter and cheese) were New Zealand's major exports while machinery, vehicles and manufactured goods were (and still remain) the major imports. At present, most trade is with countries in the **Pacific Rim** (maps **E**) – Australia, Japan, the USA and other countries in South-east Asia (the UK is still the fourth largest trading partner). Exports have diversified, with manufactured goods gaining at the expense of primary products. It has to be seen how the Asian recession of the late 1990s affects New Zealand's trade.

Activities

1 a) Explain how the information on figure **A** and diagram **B** indicate that New Zealand is wealthy and is an economically developed country.

   b) Draw two pie graphs to show New Zealand's exports and imports. Divide each graph into primary products, secondary goods, and others.

   c) Describe, with reasons, the direction of New Zealand's trade (maps **E**).

2 a) Answer Activities 1 and 2 in *Places* 107.

   b) New Zealand and Japan are both considered to be economically developed countries. In what ways does the trade of New Zealand show: i) similarities to and ii) differences from that of Japan?

3 If you have access to the Internet, you can obtain more up-to-date information on New Zealand by using the web site: http://www.odci.gov/cia/publications/factbook/ and then click onto New Zealand.

What are the main physical features of Malaysia?

Malaysia lies on a fairly stable part of the Earth's crust. It is just far enough away from the Indo-Australian and Eurasian Plate boundary not to be affected by earthquakes or volcanic eruptions (map **E** page 5). However, it was near enough for rocks originally formed on the ocean bed, like limestone, to have been pushed upwards by earth movements into high mountains (photo **A** and map **B**). In places, such as Batu to the north of Kuala Lumpur, and Niah and Mulu in Sarawak, huge caves have formed in the limestone (photo **D**). Much of Malaysia's coast, other than parts of the west of peninsular Malaysia, is undeveloped and consists of sandy beaches (photo **C**) or mangrove swamp (photo **E**).

A

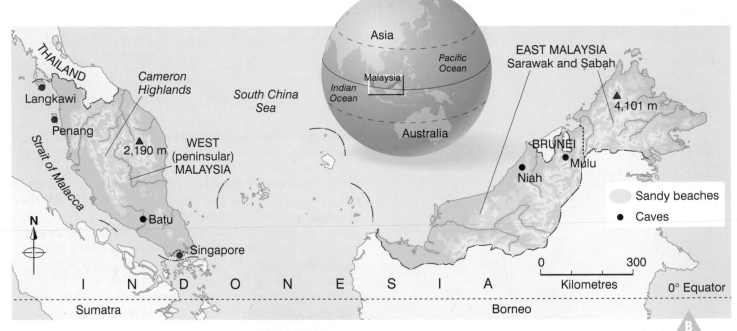

THAILAND

Cameron Highlands

Langkawi

Penang

Strait of Malacca

2,190 m

WEST (peninsular) MALAYSIA

Batu

Singapore

South China Sea

I N D O N E S I A

Sumatra

Asia

Pacific Ocean

Malaysia

Indian Ocean

Australia

EAST MALAYSIA Sarawak and Sabah

4,101 m

BRUNEI

Mulu

Niah

Sandy beaches

● Caves

0 — 300 Kilometres

0° Equator

Borneo

N

B

C

D

E

Malaysia, which lies between 1° and 7° north of the Equator, has an equatorial climate (page 34 and *Interactions* 8–9). Temperatures and humidity are high throughout the year and both the annual and daily ranges are low (figure **F**). However, it is much cooler and less humid in the mountains, and places like the Cameron Highlands have a much healthier climate than lowland areas. Rain falls throughout the year and totals everywhere exceed 2,700 mm. Most places, as in other equatorial areas, have a double rainfall maximum. These occur from March to May and from September to November when the sun is overhead (convectional rainfall, page 31). However, there is also a distinct seasonal difference between places on the coast resulting from the changing direction of the monsoon winds (*Connections* 26). Maps **G** show that coasts facing the north-east monsoon get most rain between November and April, while those facing the south-west monsoon have their peak between May and October (relief rainfall, page 31). The monsoon winds are strong and interrupt human activity (photo **H**).

The natural vegetation is tropical rainforest (photo **I** and *Interactions* 10–11). Much still remains, though deforestation, especially in eastern Malaysia, has increased rapidly in recent times.

Activities

1 a) Why do earthquakes and volcanic eruptions not occur in Malaysia?

b) Why have high mountains been formed in Malaysia?

2 a) The text refers to:
  i) annual range of temperature
  ii) diurnal range of temperature and
  iii) humidity.
  Find out what each of these three terms means.

b) Why does Malaysia have high temperatures throughout the year?

c) i) Why does Malaysia receive a double rainfall maximum?
  ii) Why do the east and west coasts of peninsular Malaysia receive most of their rainfall at different times of the year?

°C
28 July average
27 January average

2,644 Hours of sunshine (total p.a.)

Perlang
28
28

Cameron Highlands
18
18
2,492

28
24
1,673

Kuantan
2,432

Kuala Lumpur
28
27
2,218

Johor Baharu
28
27
2,034

Labuan
28
27
2,644

27
26
1,826

Kuching

0   300
Kilometres

November to April

0   300
Kilometres

May to October

0   300
Kilometres

Seasonal rainfall
Mm

Over 2,000

1,500–2,000

1,000–1,500

Under 1,000

Direction of prevailing wind

NOTICE TO SWIMMERS
MONSOON SEASON
THE SEA IS ROUGH AND DANGEROUS
SWIMMERS ARE ADVISED NOT TO SWIM
THE MANAGEMENT ACCEPTS NO
RESPONSIBILITY FOR ANY ACCIDENT
OR INJURY TO SWIMMERS WHILE
SWIMMING IN THE SEA

THE MANAGEMENT

What are the main human features of Malaysia?

The movement of people into Malaysia

- There is evidence of permanent settlement in parts of present-day Malaysia for over 10,000 years.
- In about 2500 BC, people arrived from southern China, and around 300 BC from the Indonesian islands (map **A**).
- Around AD 100, coastal settlements were set up by traders from India.

- European traders arrived from Portugal (1500s), the Netherlands (1600s) and Britain (1700s). During this time the migration of Chinese and Indians continued. Photos **B** and graph **C** show Malaysia's ethnic make-up in the mid-1990s. According to a Malaysian government handbook, 'the population of Malaysia is multi-racial, multi-cultural, multi-religious and multi-lingual'.

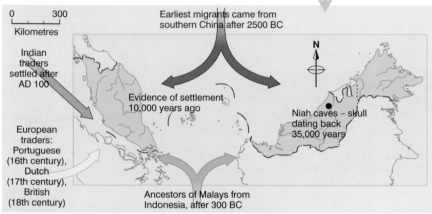

A

0 — 300 Kilometres

Earliest migrants came from southern China after 2500 BC

Indian traders settled after AD 100

Evidence of settlement 10,000 years ago

Niah caves – skull dating back 35,000 years

European traders: Portuguese (16th century), Dutch (17th century), British (18th century)

Ancestors of Malays from Indonesia, after 300 BC

N

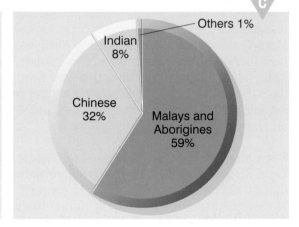

C

Others 1%

Indian 8%

Chinese 32%

Malays and Aborigines 59%

B

Distribution and density

We have already seen (page 43) that the world's population is not spread out evenly. The same is true for Malaysia. Although Malaysia's population density is increasing (from 19 per km^2 in 1950 to 64 per km^2 in 1997), its government considers that the country is **underpopulated** and could support a much larger population. The areas with both the most rapid population growth and the highest densities are located in coastal areas, especially in west peninsular Malaysia (map **D**). Most of the highlands of both peninsular and East Malaysia are sparsely populated, an exception being the Cameron Highlands area with its healthier climate (map **A** page 118).

D

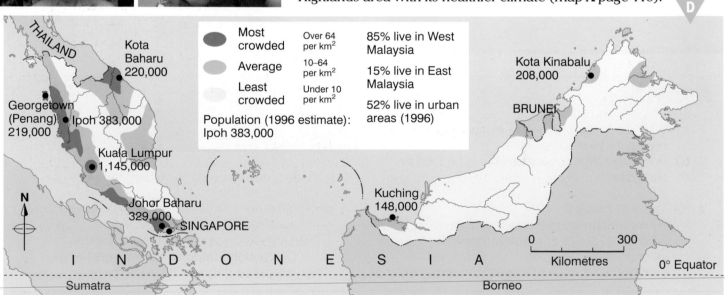

THAILAND

Kota Baharu 220,000

Georgetown (Penang) 219,000

Ipoh 383,000

Kuala Lumpur 1,145,000

Johor Baharu 329,000

SINGAPORE

	Most crowded	Over 64 per km^2
	Average	10–64 per km^2
	Least crowded	Under 10 per km^2

Population (1996 estimate): Ipoh 383,000

85% live in West Malaysia

15% live in East Malaysia

52% live in urban areas (1996)

Kota Kinabalu 208,000

BRUNEI

Kuching 148,000

N

I N D O N E S I A

0 — 300 Kilometres

0° Equator

Sumatra

Borneo

How is Malaysia's population changing?

Figure **E** shows that Malaysia's population has grown at a rapid, but steady, rate since the 1950s. This is partly because, like other economically developing countries, Malaysia has a high birth rate and, aided by a falling infant mortality rate, a high natural increase in population (page 44). What figure **E** does not show is the difference in birth rate between the main ethnic groups. This difference, mainly due to the government encouraging Malay women to 'go for five', has resulted in Malays having an average of 4.2 children per family compared with 2.4 for Indian families and 2.2 for the Chinese. Between 1980 and 1997, the proportion of Malays living in the country increased from 56 to 60 per cent (graph **C**).

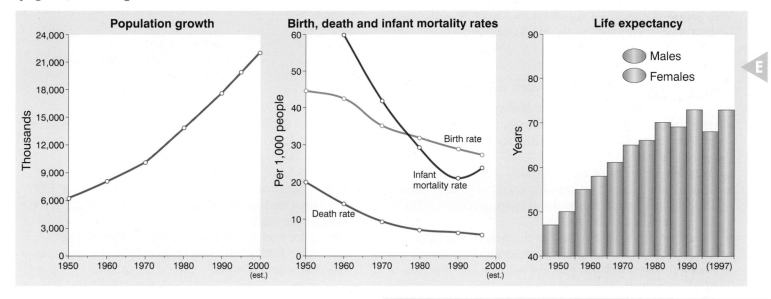

What is Malaysia's population structure?

Malaysia's population structure (graph **F**) shows that:
- Almost two out of five Malaysians (38 per cent) are aged under 15. This is relatively high even for a developing country. It is predicted that this figure is likely to remain high during the early twenty-first century as more young people (those at present under 15) enter the reproductive age-group.
- Less than one in 20 of the total population is aged 65 and over. It is predicted that the total number in this age-group will rise slowly due to the increase in life expectancy (graph **E**).

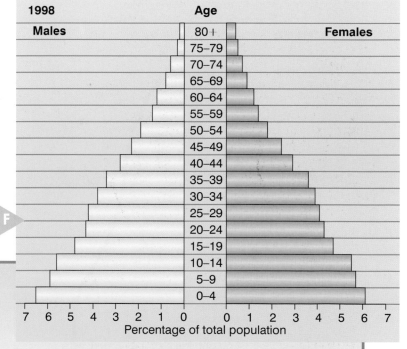

Activities

1 Study map **A** and graph **C**.
   a) Where did each of the three major ethnic groups at present living in Malaysia come from, and when did they arrive?
   b) How do you think each has influenced Malaysia's i) religious and ii) cultural life?

2 Try to find out why:
   a) most of the country's population live near to the west coast of peninsular Malaysia (think about relief, climate, resources, transport, services and interdependence with other countries)
   b) most of East Malaysia and central peninsular Malaysia are sparsely populated (think of the clues offered in a)).

3 With the help of figures **E** and **F** and page 45, describe how the shape of Malaysia's population pyramid shows that the country has i) a high birth rate ii) a high infant mortality rate iii) a high natural increase iv) a fairly short life expectancy.

What are the physical characteristics of two regions in Malaysia?

Physical similarities and differences

It is difficult to select two contrasting regions in Malaysia. For example, should a region in peninsular Malaysia be contrasted with one in East Malaysia (Sabah and Sarawak), or should a region with most economic development be contrasted with one showing less change from the traditional way of life?

Geomorphological processes and landforms

West peninsular Malaysia

- Fold mountains, rounded and reduced in height by erosion, form the eastern limits (map **A**, cross-section **B**, photo **C**).
- Uplands have not been glaciated.
- Rivers, which are relatively long, become fast-flowing after the monsoon rains and transport material from the mountains to the sea.
- Along the coast, especially to the south, the land has been extended outwards by material deposited by rivers. In the north are islands with sandy beaches.

East peninsular Malaysia

- Fold mountains, rounded and reduced in height by erosion, form the western limits (map **A** and cross-section **B**).
- Uplands have not been glaciated.
- Rivers become fast-flowing after the monsoon rains but carry less material towards the sea. Many have wide, tidal estuaries (photo **D**).
- Along the coast, the water is clear – there are extensive sandy beaches (photo **E**) and numerous offshore coral islands.

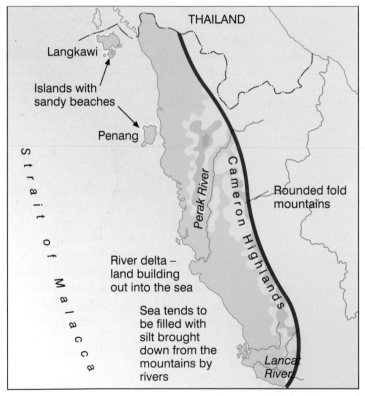

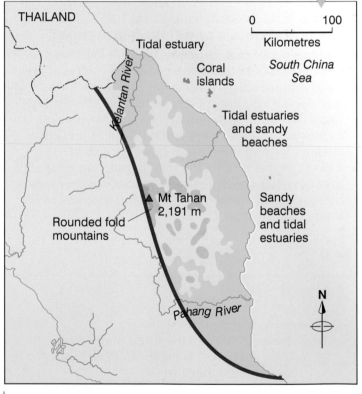

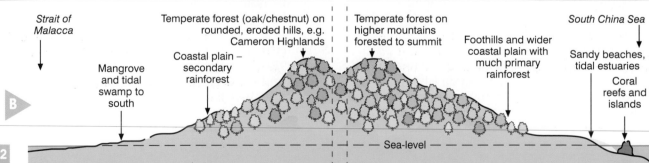

Climate

As all parts of Malaysia have an equatorial climate (pages 34, 119 and *Interactions* 8), then it is to be expected that both coasts of peninsular Malaysia will have high and constant temperatures together with heavy rainfall throughout the year (graphs **F**). Indeed the only significant difference between Penang, situated off the west coast, and Kuantan, located on the east coast, is the time of year when most rain is recorded. Penang receives most of its rainfall between August and November when the south-west monsoon winds are blowing (maps **G** page 119). In contrast the wettest time of the year in Kuantan is between November and January when the monsoon winds, having changed direction, are blowing from the north-east (maps **G** page 119).

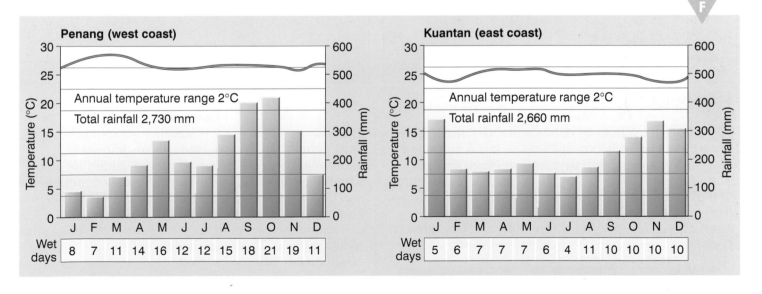

F

Penang (west coast)

Annual temperature range 2°C

Total rainfall 2,730 mm

Wet days	8	7	11	14	16	12	12	15	18	21	19	11
	J	F	M	A	M	J	J	A	S	O	N	D

Kuantan (east coast)

Annual temperature range 2°C

Total rainfall 2,660 mm

Wet days	5	6	7	7	7	6	4	11	10	10	10	10
	J	F	M	A	M	J	J	A	S	O	N	D

Activities

1 What are i) the similarities and ii) the differences in:
 a) geomorphological processes and **b)** landforms between the west of peninsular Malaysia and the east?

2 **a)** Why should it be expected that the west and east coasts of peninsular Malaysia have a similar climate?
 b) In what ways does the climate of the two regions differ?

What are the human characteristics of two regions in Malaysia?

Human and economic similarities and differences

Population

Differences in population density between the west and east of peninsular Malaysia are shown on map **D**

on page 120. The density of the western region is, however, growing far more rapidly than the east due to internal migration (**rural–urban**) and migrant workers (often illegally from nearby countries).

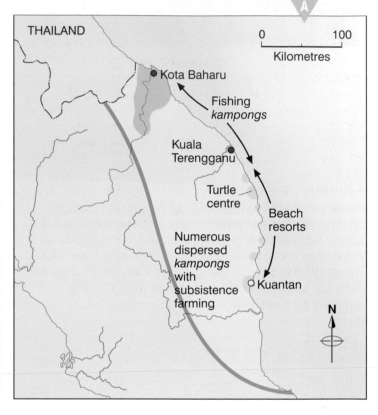

Map labels (west region):
THAILAND
Langkawi
Penang – 'Silicon Island' and tourist centre
Butterworth
Georgetown
Many commercial rubber plantations
Taiping
Ipoh
Cameron Highlands – several tourist resorts, tea-growing, fruit and vegetables
Numerous modern transport links
Shah Alam (industrial and new town)
Kuala Lumpur (capital)
Petaling Jaya
Klang (port)
Seremban

Legend:
● City/large town
○ Small town
Tourist resort/centre
Rubber-growing area
Tin (mainly exhausted)

Map labels (east region):
THAILAND
0 100 Kilometres
Kota Baharu
Fishing *kampongs*
Kuala Terengganu
Turtle centre
Beach resorts
Numerous dispersed *kampongs* with subsistence farming
Kuantan
N

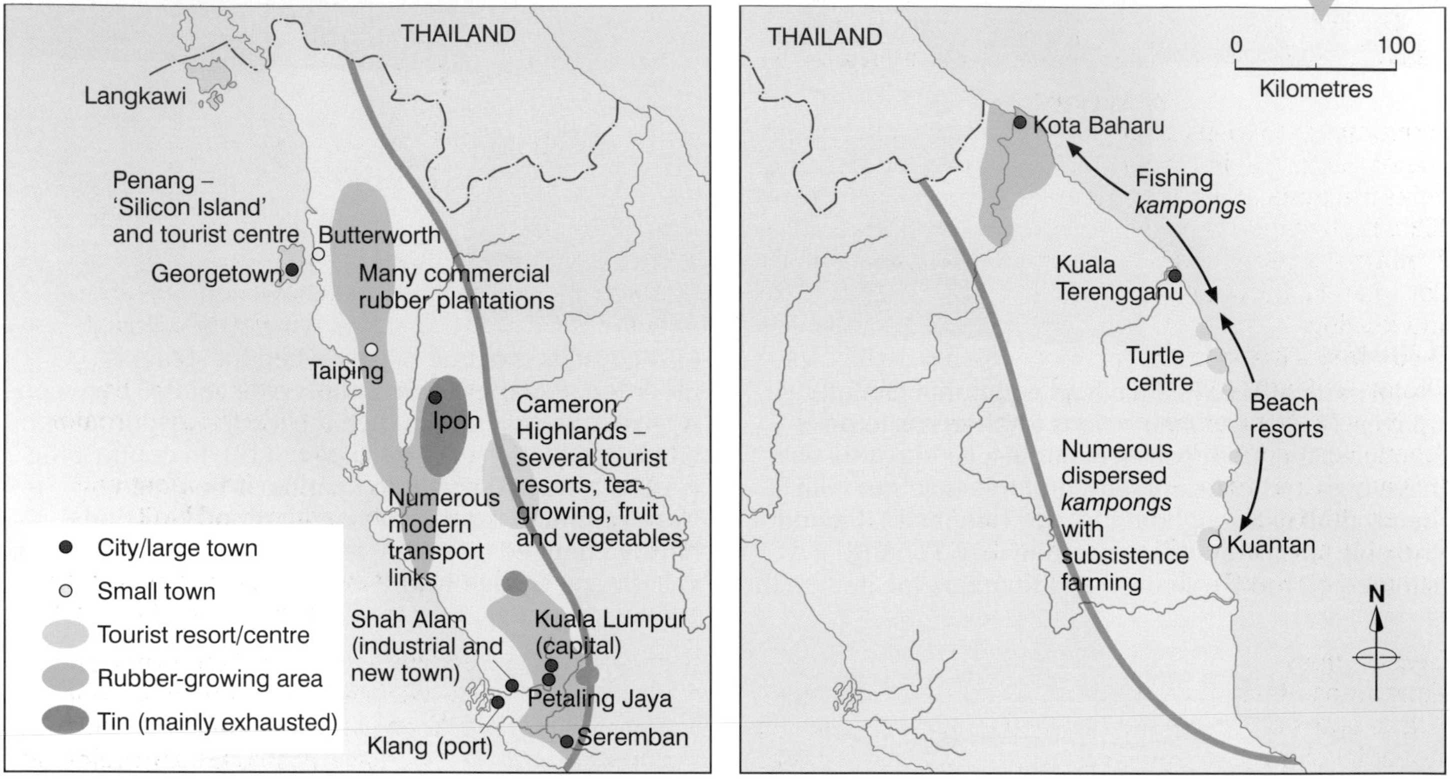

Settlement

West coast

Kuala Lumpur (photo **B**) is the capital city and largest settlement (1.15 million inhabitants). It is surrounded by several equally rapidly growing towns such as Shah Alam (photo **D**) and Petaling Jaya (map **A**). Elsewhere in the region there are numerous towns like Ipoh (once the world's tin capital), Seremban (near the new international airport), Klang (the port) and Georgetown, Penang. All are linked by a modern transport system.

East coast

The eastern region has few sizeable settlements (map **A**). Most people live in dispersed villages known as *kampongs* (photo **C**). *Kampongs* are usually located within the forest under the protection of coconut palms and banana and papaya trees, or on river estuaries. Each consists of up to twenty small, wooden communal houses built on stilts, surrounding a central meeting-place. The villagers rely on fishing, if on the coast, or subsistence farming.

Economic activities

West coast

Economic growth in this region was, during the 1990s, one of the fastest in the world. Government aim is to make Malaysia an economically developed country by 2020. High standard of living.

Primary – early development was in tin-mining areas. Commercial farming (mainly rubber – photo **E**) and logging.

Secondary – Kuala Lumpur region important with cars (Proton) at Shah Alam, textiles, pharmaceuticals, multimedia publishers, electronics and high-tech industries. Penang has become known as 'silicon island' (photo **D**).

Tertiary – many new services created in urban areas. Modern transport network, tourism and leisure around Kuala Lumpur, in the Cameron Highlands and on the islands of Penang and Langkawi.

Environment

Many areas of natural forest have either been replaced by tree crops or cleared for tin mining and, increasingly, urban development. Recent attempts have been made to restore former tin workings (photo **F**).

East coast

Economic growth in this region has been very slow with little change to the traditional way of life. High quality of life.

Primary – mainly subsistence farming (coconuts, bananas, papaya) and fishing. Development of major oilfield offshore from Terengganu.

Secondary – some food processing. Important craft industries (silverware, cloth weaving and batik making).

Tertiary – limited transport system and relatively few services. Tourism developing along parts of the coast.

There is emphasis on 'green tourism' (ecotourism) with an abundance of wildlife, unspoilt beaches and a clean sea. At Rantau Abang four types of female turtle, including the giant leatherback (photo **G**), lay their eggs (unless they are prevented by the presence of tourists).

Activity

What are i) the similarities and ii) the differences in:
a) population distribution **b)** settlement
c) economic activities and **d)** environmental protection between the west coast of peninsular Malaysia and the east coast?

How developed and how interdependent is Malaysia?

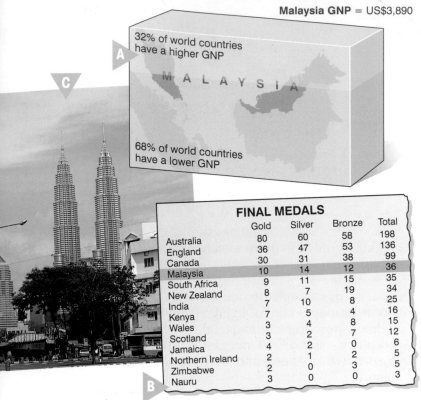

Malaysia GNP = US$3,890

A 32% of world countries have a higher GNP

C

68% of world countries have a lower GNP

FINAL MEDALS

	Gold	Silver	Bronze	Total
Australia	80	60	58	198
England	36	47	53	136
Canada	30	31	38	99
Malaysia	10	14	12	36
South Africa	9	11	15	35
New Zealand	8	7	19	34
India	7	10	8	25
Kenya	7	5	4	16
Wales	3	4	8	15
Scotland	3	2	7	12
Jamaica	4	2	0	6
Northern Ireland	2	1	2	5
Zimbabwe	2	0	3	5
Nauru	3	0	0	3

B

How developed is Malaysia?

By now you should be aware that the term **development** is not an easy one to define. To many people it means how rich a country is and how high the standard of living is for its people. The wealth of a country is given by the **gross national product (GNP)** per person, expressed in US dollars (page 76, *Interactions* 86, *Places* 7). As Malaysia does not have a particularly high GNP, it is considered to be an economically developing country, even though it is better off than two-thirds of the world's countries (map **A**). Its aim is to become 'economically developed' by the year 2020.

Development can also be measured, and described, by differences in employment (*Interactions* 86–87), trade, population, health and education (*Places* 8–11, 33, 60–61). Yet each of these measures may in turn be linked to the wealth of a country, as the richer it is the more money it will have to spend on such things as schools, hospitals and imports (figure **D**). Malaysia's recent success in trying to become more developed may be seen by its having (early 1999) the world's tallest building (photo **C**), and by its success in the 1998 Commonwealth Games, which it hosted (table **B**).

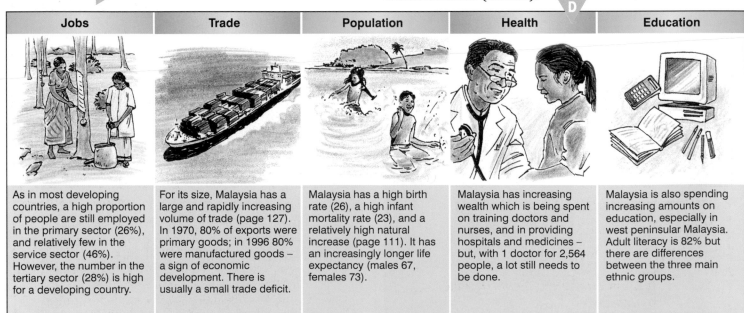

D

Jobs	Trade	Population	Health	Education
As in most developing countries, a high proportion of people are still employed in the primary sector (26%), and relatively few in the service sector (46%). However, the number in the tertiary sector (28%) is high for a developing country.	For its size, Malaysia has a large and rapidly increasing volume of trade (page 127). In 1970, 80% of exports were primary goods; in 1996 80% were manufactured goods – a sign of economic development. There is usually a small trade deficit.	Malaysia has a high birth rate (26), a high infant mortality rate (23), and a relatively high natural increase (page 111). It has an increasingly longer life expectancy (males 67, females 73).	Malaysia has increasing wealth which is being spent on training doctors and nurses, and in providing hospitals and medicines – but, with 1 doctor for 2,564 people, a lot still needs to be done.	Malaysia is also spending increasing amounts on education, especially in west peninsular Malaysia. Adult literacy is 82% but there are differences between the three main ethnic groups.

How interdependent is Malaysia?

As was explained on pages 82 and 116, all countries need to be **interdependent**, either working together or relying upon others if they are to improve their standard of living and way of life. One way by which countries become interdependent is through trade (page 82, *Interactions* 88, *Places* 58, 106).

In recent years Malaysia's trade has increased considerably although it often has a small **trade deficit** – that is, it spends more money on imports than it makes from its exports (diagram **E**).

Malaysia's imports, with less than 15 per cent being primary products, are typical of an economically developing country (map **A**). However, there has been a dramatic change in the nature of the country's exports due to its rapid economic development over the last quarter of a century. Whereas in 1970 almost 80 per cent of its exports were primary products (more typical of a developing country, e.g. Kenya, *Places* 58), by 1996 almost 80 per cent of its exports were manufactured goods (more typical of a developed country, e.g. Japan, *Places* 106).

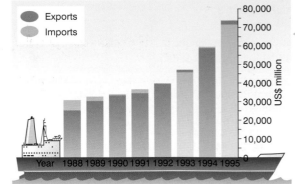

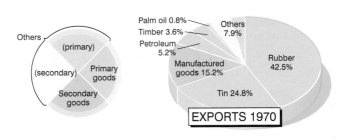

EXPORTS 1970

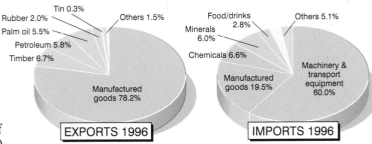

EXPORTS 1996   IMPORTS 1996

Until the 1970s most of Malaysia's exports, two-thirds of which were rubber and tin, went to the UK (diagram **F**). At the same time many of its imports, most of which were (and still are) manufactured goods, machinery and transport equipment, also came from the UK. Since then:

- the direction of trade has altered, with the UK joining the EU and Malaysia trading with other **Pacific Rim** countries (maps **G**)

- the type of exports from Malaysia has changed from primary products (a decline in world demand for rubber and tin) to manufactured goods (a growth in world demand for electronics and other high-tech goods).

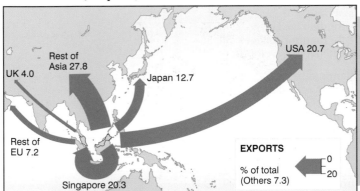

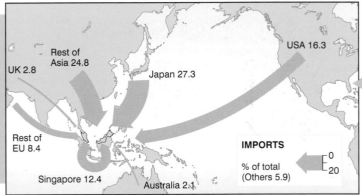

Activities

1 **a)** Explain how the information on figures **A** to **F** indicates that:
   i) Malaysia is an economically developing country
   ii) Malaysia is economically more developed than many developing countries.

   b) Draw two pie graphs to show Malaysia's exports and imports. Divide each graph into primary products, secondary goods, and others.

   c) Describe, with reasons, the direction of Malaysia's trade (maps **G**).

2 **a)** Make sure that you can answer Activities 1 and 2 in *Places* 107.

   b) Malaysia and Kenya are both considered to be economically developing countries. In what ways does the trade of Malaysia show:
   i) similarities to and ii) differences from that of Kenya? (You will need to consult *Places* 58–59 to answer this question.)

3 If you have access to the Internet, you can obtain more up-to-date information on Malaysia by using the web site at:
   http://www.odci.gov/cia/publications/factbook
   and then click onto Malaysia.

Index